Organizations and Complex Adaptive Systems

Organizations and Complex Adaptive Systems explains complexity theory within the organizational studies and discusses the applicability of complex adaptive systems principles for intraorganizational and interorganizational levels.

Complex adaptive systems and complexity theory have been studied in many different fields of science. When studying the application of complex adaptive systems within social sciences, not many are seen in real terms in contrary to the myriads of theories and propositions available. The complex adaptive systems perspective is presented in quantitative terms in natural sciences, but a quantitative approach has not been used within social sciences a lot comparatively. This book links the basics of complex adaptive systems to social sciences, focusing on organizational studies and covering interorganizational, organizational, and individual levels.

It shows the latest state of knowledge on the topic and will be of interest to researchers, academics, managers, and students in the fields of management, organizational theory and behavior, and strategic management.

Mahsa Fidanboy received her Ph.D. in Management and Organization from Ankara Yıldırım Beyazıt University, Social Sciences Institute, and is a professional consultant with Fidanboy Consulting, Turkey.

Routledge Focus on Business and Management

The fields of business and management have grown exponentially as areas of research and education. This growth presents challenges for readers trying to keep up with the latest important insights. *Routledge Focus on Business and Management* presents small books on big topics and how they intersect with the world of business research.

Individually, each title in the series provides coverage of a key academic topic, whilst collectively, the series forms a comprehensive collection across the business disciplines.

The Multiple Case Study Design
Methodology and Application for Management Education
Daphne Halkias, Michael Neubert, Paul W. Thurman and Nicholas Harkiolakis

Organizations, Strategic Risk Management and Resilience
The Impact of Covid-19 on Tourism
Patrizia Gazzola, Enrica Pavione and Ilaria Pessina

Organizations and Complex Adaptive Systems
Mahsa Fidanboy

Managing Complexity in Healthcare
Lesley Kuhn and Kieran Le Plastrier

Work Organizational Reforms and Employment Relations in the Automotive Industry
American Employment Relations in Transition
Kenichi Shinohara

For more information about this series, please visit: www.routledge.com/ Routledge-Focus-on-Business-and-Management/book-series/FBM

Organizations and Complex Adaptive Systems

Mahsa Fidanboy

Routledge
Taylor & Francis Group

NEW YORK AND LONDON

First published 2022
by Routledge
605 Third Avenue, New York, NY 10158

and by Routledge
4 Park Square, Milton Park, Abingdon, Oxon, OX14 4RN

Routledge is an imprint of the Taylor & Francis Group, an informa business

© 2022 Mahsa Fidanboy

Library of Congress Cataloging-in-Publication Data
Names: Fidanboy, Masha, author.
Title: Organizations and complex adaptive systems / Dr. Masha Fidanboy.
Description: New York, NY : Routledge, 2022. |
Includes bibliographical references and index.
Identifiers: LCCN 2022006230 | ISBN 9781032022932 (hardback) |
ISBN 9781032022956 (paperback) | ISBN 9781003182764 (ebook)
Subjects: LCSH: Social sciences–Methodology. |
Quantitative research. | Strategic planning.
Classification: LCC H61 .F46 2022 | DDC 300.1–dc23/eng/20220214
LC record available at https://lccn.loc.gov/2022006230

ISBN: 978-1-03-202293-2 (hbk)
ISBN: 978-1-03-202295-6 (pbk)
ISBN: 978-1-00-318276-4 (ebk)

DOI: 10.4324/9781003182764

Typeset in Times New Roman
by Newgen Publishing UK

To my all, my son, Vedat Ozan
and
my grandparents, Babaji and Mamaryam,
my mom, my sister, and my husband

Contents

1 System

System, a word which we use and hear in our everyday life, is used in many different situations and contexts, not in variant meanings, but all in almost similar or close senses despite the level of complexity of the situation. What we generally mean by the system is the whole consisting of the parts of which each has a function that might be similar or different from the functions of the other parts, and all parts follow the goals(s) determined for the system. The easiest example is our body consisting of many parts called organs with the common goal of making the system live in spite of the malfunctions they show from time to time that may not satisfy the common goal. In this example, the proximity of the parts to each other is seen even though this is not same for all the systems, for instance, the health system of a country. It subsumes all health organizations and health workers even at the farthest part located from the capital. Thus, the geographical distance is not a barrier on the way to consider a part away from the other parts as part of a system. An example in the context of business organizations can be a main company with several branches located worldwide which altogether form a bigger system. Besides the proximity of the parts, the function(s) of each part should also be paid attention to. As in the healthcare system, a cleaning staff in a hospital has different tasks from a surgeon though their common goal is to deliver the health services to the people, and when viewing from the system point, the parts, regardless of their functions, are all committed to reach the goals of the system. Furthermore, looking back at the example again makes us think of the different levels present within a system, the health workers as the individual, the hospitals and health institutes as the organizations, and the national health system as part of the worldwide health system. Given all mentioned, the key points to be focused on when talking of a system can be listed as follows:

1   The proximity and location of the parts
2   The functions of the parts
3   The main goal(s) of the system
4   The levels nested in the system
5   The interactions both between the parts and among the different levels.

DOI: 10.4324/9781003182764-1

This can help in defining the system as a whole consisting of many parts in direct or indirect relationship with each other, and all serve the system to reach its common goal.

Classification as a method to distinguish and explore the dissimilar characteristics of different groups can be used here too. Systems can be divided into two separate groups: open and closed systems. These two systems are well-defined in the natural sciences such as chemistry by explaining the concepts of enthalpy and entropy. To describe them in a nutshell, enthalpy is the sum of the internal energy in a system while entropy refers to the level of disorder in the system. Viewing them from the standpoint of social sciences, enthalpy, the exchange of energy and work can be represented as the resources provided to an organization which can be in any of its forms such as human resources, financial resources, and so on. As for entropy, the disorder in the organization can be perceived similarly in its general usage, and changes of the disorder level result in different states in an organization including 'order,' 'chaos,' and between these, at the edge of 'chaos,' rests 'complexity' (Dodder & Dare, 2000). The level of disorder is the lowest in the order state, increases when moving from order to complexity, and from complexity to chaos, reaching its highest point at the chaos state.

The perspective used in this book is a complex adaptive systems (CAS) perspective which consider the systems as both complex and adaptive at the same time, each of which will be elucidated in the following chapters. In a nutshell, complex systems are systems made of many connected and interacting parts. With respect to the adaptive systems, four components were suggested for them – sensor, adjustment mechanism and controller, actuator, and feedback and adaptation loops, which are all needed for the system to be adaptive (George & Lin, 2017). A model was presented in the same article consisting of these components in accordance with the control systems approach. From a CAS standpoint, adaptive systems are the systems able to adapt themselves to the changes in their environments, and according to the literature, they possess learning capabilities (Stacey, 1996).

Organizational Level

When putting the organizations under lenses at different levels of study, the properties of the system are needed to be defined each time accordingly. The organizational level study of the organizations as complex adaptive systems will have some similarities with organizational studies of the same level, although the differences root from the perspective from which the system is viewed from. The organization from a CAS viewpoint has an organic structure that supplies the organization with the flexibility required in order to be adaptive at the time of changes. The other perspectives may deem the organizations with mechanistic structure, unable to change or adapt. These perspectives are mainly among the ones ignoring the adaptation, but regarding the selection as the key impact of environment on the organization.

In addition, the organization is a whole consisting of physical and non-physical assets, and all can be taken as parts of a system when being taken into consideration from other perspectives, yet the individuals are the main focus of the CAS perspective in the context of the social sciences.

Individuals

Among the numerous parts of an organization, the individuals are the key role players from a CAS standpoint. These individuals, in order to be considered in the system, should bear some characteristics which are explained in the following.

First of all, they should be in interactions with each other to a high level (Anderson, 1999; Tan, Wen, & Awad, 2005). By interactions, communication can be perceived simply; however, when looking at it more carefully, the action and the reaction can be more meaningful concerning its perception; an individual acts and another individual reacts to it, and vice versa. The action of the individual which then triggers the reaction might have either direct or indirect impact on the reactive responses. These can be clarified with some examples. In a software development company, a customer requested for the conformity of an ongoing software project to a new quality standard. The project manager is needed to adjust the project's cost, time, and scope to the new requirements, and his reactions have been directly influenced by the change request. After the approval of the changes by the project manager and the top management, the changes are communicated to the development team to act accordingly. The customer decision is taken as the trigger action, and the conformity of the team is the last reaction that was affected indirectly through the mediator role of the changes of the project attributes. The direct or indirect nature of the impact can be determined this way: If the action forces the changes on the other action without any mediators, the impact is taken as direct; however, in the situation where an action changes the context for performance of the other action, the impact is regarded indirect. Identifying the chain of interactions enables us to specify the triggers, changes, and notably the dynamics of a system. In relation to this, two not-apparent-blurred-bordered mindsets come up: taking the changes as a cycle or considering them as a chain. The chain cannot be necessarily a finite one, and when it is infinite, the determination of its future path, whether it is going back to its initial point which makes it a cycle, would not be easy to trace. This may result in the usage of the cycle and chain words interchangeably in some cases.

In addition to the interactions between the parts, the system interacts with its environment as well (Oughton, Usher, Tyler, & Hall, 2018). CAS is a kind of open systems; the systems which exchange energy and information with the environment surrounding them (Ali, 2015). The environment outside, beyond the borders of a system, can be decomposed into immediate and universal environment. The immediate environment is the part in close contact with the system, and it is posited in a bigger environment itself, the universal environment. Taking a hospital as the system, the national health organizations can be its immediate environment, and all the international health organizations make the universal environment. From another point of view, for a hospital in a small town, the town can be perceived as the immediate environment and the country can be assumed in the role of the universal environment. In line with the purpose of the study, several environments might be identified which they may be nested in each other or having parts in common with the other environments or unique to themselves; nevertheless, all are part of the universal environment. The changes can be imposed on the system from the environment or the other way around. Although the environment is bigger than the system in size, or we may say it is infinite, the changes that the system pushes toward the environment can be small but still effective enough to make changes to the environment. From a CAS perspective, even a small change should be taken into consideration as it may lead to remarkable changes in the future of the system.

The second characteristic of the individuals is the interdependencies between them and as a whole with the larger environment (Anderson, 1999; Tan, Wen, & Awad, 2005). The interdependencies between the components of the system restrict their freedom. Interestingly, reducing or increasing the levels of freedom of the components of a system plays an important role in the determination of its level of complexity as well as the scale whether small or large (Siegenfeld & Bar-Yam, 2020). If the freedom given to the agents is low, they may have less options regarding the behavior they will show in response to the changes. This will probably restrict their degrees of creativity and innovation. In contrast, when the agents have much freedom, more than the ideal level, they will behave in every possible way, regardless of the history of the system and the decisions of other agents. This will end with chaos which is not a favorable state for the organizations. Besides, understanding the tradeoff between complexity and scale can assist in making decisions on narrowing the scope of manufacturing or widening it.

Similar to the interdependencies between the components of the system, interdependency with the environment exists to different extents. Being too interdependent with the environment means more efforts needed to be made to conform to the changes, and if done successfully, it actually implies more adaptability. The less a system is interdependent with its environment, the less it is impacted from it which then enables the firm to act more freely. This situation can be either hazardous or beneficial to the firm, depending on the many visible and invisible factors. It is like just a situation at which a technology company introduces a new gadget to the market. The outcome of the radical innovation when the firm has its own way of thinking and making, irrespective of what is imposed on it from the environment, will vary, bringing about two possible cases; the new gadget may become either so popular or a huge disappointment. This is the exact point at which the famous questions arises; 'adapt or not to adapt, if yes, so to what extent?'

The third characteristic of the individuals is acting in unpredictable ways by using their freedom (Van Eijnatten, 2004). This unpredictability exists in the long term, but not in the short term (Schueler, 1996). In the case of the individuals as parts of the system, predicting the behavior and the decision of them can be possible if the predictions are being made for a short time, close to now. However, foreseeing the outcomes, the further future might not be as easy as it seems to be. The sensitivity to initial conditions makes the situation harder for predictions due to the fact that even a small change in the behavior of an individual or a decision slightly different from the previous ones can lead to completely different conditions in the future.

The fourth characteristic of the individuals is their ability to research, learn, self-organize, and adapt to the changes in their environments at various levels (Carlisle & McMillan, 2006). It is noteworthy that the environment plays a key role in the adaptation of an organization. Even if the sources seem to root in the decision of a manager or the implementation of a new procedure, the main reason is the environment definitely. In the previous examples, some changes in the environment might have triggered the change of strategy in a firm or the need for the modification of the procedures. Apart from the impact of the environment, the agents' capabilities should also be taken into account. The critical capability for adaptation is learning. What is seen in the real world cases is that not all employees are willing to learn, and not all of those who are willing to learn, learn at the same speed with the others. Even the amount of what they learn during a certain amount of time varies which is the reason why for some job positions, being a quick learner is included as the characteristics of the individuals the companies are looking for. Particularly, learning becomes so momentous when the nature of environment is highly dynamic and turbulent.

Agents

Agents were referred to as the bases of a CAS (Dooley, 1996). Agents attempt to be fitted with their environment through adaptation, which then leads to the evolution of the overall system over time. They were labeled as 'semi-autonomous' (Dooley, 1996). This can be interpreted as having the freedom to decide how to behave, though being located in the context of a system puts some restrictions on the range or the depth of their choices. It can be considered true for all agents in a system as they are all part of a whole, interconnected with other agents, not as isolated elements. In the organizational studies, these agents can also be called as decision makers or the decision-making entities due to their decision-making ability. It should not be overlooked that as the systems can be considered differently in accordance with the level of study, the same condition is also valid for the agents. Agents may be persons, a team, a department, a business unit, or even the organization as a whole (Choi, Dooley, & Rungtusanatham, 2001). The most interesting and hard-to-measure part of CAS is the rules these agents act according to. These rules originate from a 'mental template' (Dooley, 1996) or a 'cognitive structure' (Anderson, 1999) which form and determine the rules the behavior comes from.

Schemata

Each agent has its own way of interpreting the environment and the situation with which he/she encounters, and consequently, his/her perception of the environment may differ from another agent's perception even if all the factors related to the situation can be taken as fixed. The difference or the resemblance comes from the agent's schema. To be clear, the cognitive structure according to which the agents behave may differ among different agents or they may be same (Eisenhardt & Bhatia, 2005; Anderson, 1999). The difference between the schemata may be even seen at the upper levels, for example, in the organizations (Stacey, 1996). These schemata provide us with descriptions of the situations along with both predictions and prescriptions (Gell-Mann, 1994). Each of these three notions bear remarkable importance; the descriptions are specially needed for the righteous perception of the situation currently faced. The predictions are done for the new situations rise, the ones not encountered before. The decisions for these new situations are made based on the current situation of the system, together with using the cumulative knowledge and experience of the decision makers through the years whether at the same organization or not. These decisions are accompanied by prescriptions since predicting will not suffice when solutions are not to be suggested. To sum up, the schemata not only affect the current behavior of the system but also have an influence on the future of the system. One point should not be neglected here which is about the decision maker. The decision makers who have been working at the same organization for a long time should be careful with not being trapped into the locked-in situation resulted from being so path-dependent. A completely opposite condition may exist for the decision makers newly started at an organization facing the risk of taking decisions that are not in line with the previous ones along with the history of the organization, using the CAS terminology, the case of low path-dependency which will also bring drawbacks to the system.

Schemata might be hard to comprehend when being viewed as a cognitive structure, instead they can be interpreted as a guidance for the actions which define the limits of the actions, prioritizing them, assigning them time, and representing a how-to guide for the actions (Eisenhardt & Bhatia, 2005; Eisenhardt & Sull, 2001). The schemata not only influence the actions of the agents but also have an impact on the interactions between them by determining their rules (Dooley, 1997). These interactions are in the form of the exchange of information and resources. This can be clarified within an example. Two different departments of an organization managed by two persons who can be labeled as agents share the information on their progresses, impediments, delays in their plans, etc., with each other. This is not limited to the information only, and in some cases they may share their resources like their staff or reassign budgets among their projects.

Apart from the individual approach to schemata, there exists a collective approach toward them where the schemata are defined as the beliefs, norms, values, as well as the assumptions held commonly by a group of people; for instance, the norms and beliefs held among the employees of an organization or a group of organizations working as the branches of a headquarter can be looked on as the organizational schemata. Hence, when studying the schemata, the aforementioned factors should not a disregarded, and this implies that the organizational culture should be concentrated on the related studies. Looking at the literature provides some interesting examples on the importance of schemata in practice. As an example, if a buyer and a supplier have common schemata, the communication taken place between them will be more efficient, and the transaction costs will decrease (Choi, Dooley, & Rungtusanatham, 2001). Likewise, the implementation of international quality standards, models, and frameworks will bring about the benefits of sharing the common schemata. This will be explained in detail in Chapter 4.

Till now, the individual schemata and the collective schemata have been mentioned as well as the factors affecting them, although a kind of schema seems to be missing, the one related to the strategies and plans of the system (McCarthy, 2003). Being a part of a system does alter the schemata in a way to be fitted with the goals of the system. The impact might vary from an agent to the other, and it is predicted to be associated with the organizational identification and the organizational commitment. Taking all the above-mentioned factors into consideration, the schemata can be categorized under three different groups: individual, collective, and strategic which can be the focus of studies compliant with their relevant level. In order to predict the behavior of a system, the rules of each of these categories and their effects on each other are needed to be extracted and interpreted.

In order to model the schemata, the rules need to be identified and recorded in the form of verbal rules or in the form of mathematical algorithms. As schemata embrace three different sections, the descriptions, the predictions, and the prescriptions (Gell-Mann, 1994), each statement or the mathematical instruction of the model can be marked as one of these. What should not be forgotten about the schemata is their rational bounded nature due to the biased or incomplete information (Dooley, 1996). To put it in other words, since the schema is a cognitive structure and the human is rationally bounded, the schema will bear the same property of being bounded rationally.

Behavior

The behavior is shown as an outcome of the schemata, and this is the reason why studying the schemata is of high significance for the prediction of behavior. How these rules work can be summarized into three steps (Nan, 2011): inspection, execution, and fitness in agreement with the positive or negative feedbacks. By the continuance of repetition of these steps or it can be said as iteration, each time that a decision is being made, the agents learn from their experience, and that is why a CAS is a learning system. The learning process helps the agents to adapt to their environment. This includes both the environment outside the border of the system and also the part in the system which is altered from time to time resulting from the actions of the other agents. Therefore, the behavior is shaped mutually, and this mutually developed adaptive behavior is called as interaction (Nan, 2011).

The levels of a CAS are nested or, to say it differently, there exists the inclusion of a system in another. Similar to the schemata and in the same line with it, the behavior can be categorized as the behavior of the individual, the collective behavior, and the strategic behavior. Based on the situation involved in, the behavior that is indicated may be one or some of these, or a new behavior rooting from the combination and consideration of all.

Interorganizational Level

Widening the locus of focus of study from the organizations to the interorganizational level necessitates the concentration on how organizations interact with each other, and the answers to several questions are sought: How do organizations exchange information and resources with each other? How often and to what extent is this flow seen? How is the direction of this flow most of the time? How are the relationships between organizations? Do they compete against each other or do they collaborate together? To what extent are competition and collaboration seen between the organizations? While answering these questions, some issues should not be turned a blind eye to. The first is that in cases where an organization control the market and has a dominant position like what is in a monopoly market, the competition or collaboration might seem to get faded but they actually exist. The extent to which these two take place may differ from time to time, and from case to case, but they may not become zero in practice. An example can help with the understanding of this statement. Suppose there is only one TV manufacturer in a country and there are no imports from other countries as well. The market is a monopoly. A smartphone manufacturer starts to produce phones with bigger screens and sells its phones with a free video streaming application already installed on them. At first glance, a TV manufacturer does not assume a smartphone manufacturer as a rival; nonetheless, as the time passes, it indicates that the time of watching videos on TV is decreasing drastically whereas the time of watching on a smartphone has been rocketed to the top. This can imply that even in a blue ocean, a breeze can make waves that can gradually turn into a storm. Living in a dynamic world makes it unavoidable to compete or for those who are reluctant to use the word 'competition,' it will be impossible to ignore what others are doing and refuse to take the next steps according to the acts of the others. That is what being part of a system means, not being isolated, but being intertwined with the system.

The second issue is that competition and collaboration may coexist although in some situations one will be too low to be noticed. This is the desire for competition and collaboration which push the organizations toward the choice of forming alliances, joint ventures, and horizontal or vertical integrations. What matters is to put a mile, or miles of distance, between the organization and its rivals, and as already known, this is not a kind of paving the path for the rivals, yet using some strategies to slow them down or even stop them from progressing such as creating market entry barriers.

The third issue is the competition, either positive or negative. Though the negative and positive competitions have been mostly highlighted among the individuals, the same notion can be utilized for the organizations similarly. Sometimes the efforts of an organization to overcome its rival are destructive to the point that it worsens the situation for all who are present in the market, even itself. Hence, when competing, the consequences of the actions which are going to be taken must always be anticipated and estimated for they may at last return to the actors themselves since all of them are part of a macro system, and any changes, even the mild ones, have the potential to cause catastrophic results.

In order to investigate how the relationships between the organizations are and work, first, the context at which they are posited should be determined; whether they have built clusters with the ones in the same industry or if they are part of a network or to be more precise and plain, which economic agglomerations they have formed with other organizations. Studying the organizations in their contexts is what is prescribed by CAS perspective for the reasons that first, the elements of the system are not separate from each other, oppositely, they are interdependent with each other, and second, the system is an open system which is interdependent with its environment.

Clusters

What is defined as a cluster is the concentration of the firms geographically for the purpose of obtaining some kind of benefits. Among the various economic agglomerations, clusters are the ones embracing organizations from the same industry, and what the force behind this formation is stated to be innovation (Boja, 2011) or, elsewhere in literature, knowledge accumulation (Malmberg, Solvell, & Zander, 1996). Though the two are not the same actually, the first element of knowledge accumulation at the local level was suggested to be in connection with the innovation process (Malmberg, Solvell, & Zander, 1996). The advantages of being a member of a cluster are not limited to the development of the organization, fostering innovation, increased competition, external economies, and joint actions (Carpinetti, Galdamez, & Gerolamo, 2008). In some countries, governments have allocated special sites to the firms making them gather together with the view to forming clusters. In addition to this allocation, extra benefits are presented to the firms such as tax exemption and financial support in order to foster the growth in the number of the firms as well as the formation of clusters which subsequently is expected to increase the level of innovation.

Looking back at the literature, some characteristics presumed to be common between clusters are the existence of linkages between firms within a cluster, the exchange of information among them, the presence of an institutional infrastructure that backs the activities of the cluster, and forming and sharing social and cultural identities which are based on their common values (Carpinetti, Galdamez, & Gerolamo, 2008; Altenburg & Meyer-Stamer, 1999). Additionally, elsewhere in the literature, external economies and joint actions were suggested as the other characteristics of clusters (Carpinetti, Galdamez, & Gerolamo, 2008). To be clearer, external economies are the savings in the costs gained from the geographical concentration of the firms originating from specialization, knowledge transfer, and innovation (Dayasindhu, 2002).

Clusters were modeled under four different categories in terms of the role of the members and their interactions (Markusen, 1996). In order to decide the type of cluster, the existence of hub firms and how firms are related need to be inspected. Some of the questions rise in the relevant studies are as follows: What are the sizes of the firms? Are there any hub firms? Hub firms are dominant firms with which some other firms are connected directly, situating them in a center of the connections (Boja, 2011); Are there any branches or parent firms or state-related organizations in the cluster? Regardless of the type of the cluster, firms are in collaboration and competition with each other. Taking either a cluster or the organizations in a cluster as agents denotes the fact that not all the agents have impact on the system equally. This matters even more when there is a hub firm or a state-related firm present in the cluster, affecting the system more than the other agents do. This casts light on why the identification of the agents is not sufficient for the CAS studies; nevertheless, the impact of the agents is required to be specified in the system.

Getting into more details concerning clusters, first, the industrial clusters embrace firms from a set of industries which are somehow related to each other (Reveiu & Dardala, 2012) which bear some remarkable characteristics subsuming foreign ownership, the dynamic nature of cluster, having a share in that country's export (Birkinshaw & Hood, 2000), generalized reciprocity, flexible specialization, and external economies (Dayasindhu, 2002). The relationships between the industries might root from what are common between them such as common buyers, suppliers, technologies, distribution channels, or labors (Reveiu & Dardala, 2012; Porter, 1990).

Regional cluster is a kind of industrial cluster at which the companies from a common or related industries gather in a specific region (Reveiu & Dardala, 2012). The characteristics of regional clusters can be summarized as the gathering of firms of specific sectors in small spatially concentrated areas which is accompanied by the formation of local production network where the flexible production methods are used within the firms, and some of the firms are active in dominant industries, and some, not all are regional innovation systems (Isaksen, 1996).

The most interesting fact about the clusters is that the competition and collaboration exist simultaneously in the clusters (Boja, 2011). Being posited at the same place makes the companies more aware of their competitors' activities. Even if they may not know fully what the other companies are doing, feeling the presence of a rival makes them work harder to exceed the others. On the other side, the proximity in terms of the space makes the collaboration more possible and easier. For instance, a software company needs a special license for one of their software programs and a firm just nearby is the provider and distributor of that program. The spatial closeness makes the company to prefer the nearby firm as it naturally seems more available in the case of the occurrence of any kind of problems. The examples might not only be restricted to the provision and supply of goods but also entailing services. In one of the cases, an education company once encountered a problem with its online education website. They were just the users of the program and they called whom they had purchased the program from for solving the problem. The seller company told them that the solution might take a few days to be presented since their technical team was working on another urgent problem. The education company then decided to ask one of the coders of the neighbour firms to see whether he could solve the problem or not and it worked. The examples of competition and collaboration within clusters are far more than can be discussed; nevertheless, the first step to take is to decide whether the companies have formed any kind of clusters or not. It is also noteworthy that sometimes collaboration might not be present as clearly as it was depicted here, though, it will be through the specialization.

Similar to organizations that can gain competitive advantage, the clusters can bear competitive advantages too. Two types of interdependencies-based characteristics of the clusters can turn into competitive advantages for them: traded and non-traded interdependencies where the first one is in respect of formal exchange of economic value and the second is related to the share of knowledge (Niu, 2010).

Networks

The word 'network' can be interpreted in many different ways. It can be described as the relationships formed between agents themselves, or between the agents and resources, or the agents and tasks, or the agents and the knowledge (Carley, 2005) formed horizontally or vertically; horizontal relationships are constructed between an organization and others all at the same phase of the supply chain, for instance, the merger of two companies doing the same business or the merger of two companies active in close complementary businesses, and vertical relationships are shaped between the organizations from the different phases(levels) of the supply chain mainly consisting of customers and suppliers. Taking into consideration the levels of study, the agents can also point to the individuals, organizations, a group of organizations, or the economy of a country as well. This highlights the importance of the determination of the agents in the system due to the fact that the relationships and the networks are defined successively.

There are rules for the formation of the networks, and these rules consider different characteristics of agents posited within the network like the centrality or the connectivity degree (Schweitzer, Fagiolo, Sornette, Vega-Redondo, & White, 2009). These agents may collaborate or compete with the other agents in the network, and at the interorganizational level, the determination of these types of relationships helps to understand the flow of information and the resources much better. What should not be neglected here is the fact that there will not be only the signs of competition or collaboration in a specific relationship, nevertheless, they may coexist with each other at the same time. This might be a bit surprising although possible, for instance, moderate levels of collaboration and competition were seen in the research conducted on the techno-parks in Ankara, Turkey (Fidanboy, 2020). One question raised here is 'to what extent the collaboration and competition can coexist' or, to put it differently, 'does being more involved in competition have any kind of influence on the degree of collaborating or not?' Even as individuals, we sometimes make choices of collaboration with the ones we compete with in order to increase our chance of becoming successful or achieving more success. Other examples can be taking the bests into your team for a project despite the fact that those bests are our rivals as well. It is also seen in the academia where two or more strong academicians gather to collaborate on an academic work. This collaboration may bring dozens of benefits to the parties; the parties might not need to assign too many resources to the tasks compared to when they are doing the tasks on their own since the resources are shared among them; the parties will be able to free up their time and their resources, therefore, they can concentrate on doing other tasks or accepting other projects too; and what is really important is the risk mitigation for the reason that the risks taken are shared between the parties or we might say that the impact of the risks will be lessened due to the division between individuals. Apart from the financial benefits resulting from the risk mitigation, it also helps the parties to be more assured and confident in their decisions and activities, and at the individual level, it reduces their stress level, affecting their well-being at their jobs. Like any other concept, collaborations may not be without drawbacks when it is not performed in the right desired way. In some situations, collaboration becomes the source of stress to individuals like when the disagreements and disputes remain unsolved or when the individuals' only attempts turn to proving themselves right and the others wrong on the argued subject. At the organizational level, the collaboration fails to be fruitful especially when the schemata regarding the collaboration have not been shared between the parties.

Likewise, the competition may have advantages or drawbacks. It can work as a motivator, fostering the agents to perform their tasks in the best way in the shortest time, even though excessing its threshold will result in exhaustion, disappointment, and demotivation. The aforementioned threshold varies from agent to agent and depends on their capacities to outperform their rivals. Along with the capacity, the duration of the competition plays an important role alike. The urge to compete for a long time may cause burnout in both the individuals and the organizations. A host of companies have failed while trying hard to catch the latest technologies or reaching a desired level of quality due to the long time it took for them to reach a certain goal, and then, another goal was headed toward, necessitating constant efforts continuously, making them struggle for a long time which would eventually lead to a burnout situation at the end, and, at worst, endanger the survival of the organization.

When talking of network, like any other concepts, the quality of it comes to mind. What is perceived from the quality of a network can range widely and its quality can be identified in numerous ways such as the benefits it provides its organizations with or the frequency and density of communications taking place in the network. The number of organizations found in a network might have an influence on the quality of the network as well. Each network may be in some ways similar to or different from the other networks. Hence, it is essential to define the characteristics a network bears at the first step of each study. The relational characteristics of a network were suggested as the network structure, tie modality, and the membership of it (Gulati, Nohria, & Zaheer, 2000; Galaskiewicz & Zaheer, 1999). Each of these characteristics can be explained and operationalized in line with the purpose of the study being conducted. For the purpose of this book and to combine the network and CAS perspectives, the network structure can be interpreted as the general pattern of the relationships between the agents, and in the case where the level of study is organizational, it points at the interorganizational relationships. By tie modality, a set of rules and norms behind the behavior of the members of network are implied. From a combined viewpoint, it can be explained as the network context-related rules and when talking of the rules of behavior, schemata come to mind which further make it possible to call it as the network schemata. The last characteristic to discuss is the network membership including everything related to the composition of a network, and in application of a merged standpoint, it includes some of the main concepts such as agents, their level of impact on the network, and the flows of information and energy.

Given all mentioned, it can be realized that the networks of relationships affect the performance and the conduct of the organizations positioned within (Gulati, Nohria, & Zaheer, 2000). What is noteworthy here is that the positive effects of being situated in a network cannot be guaranteed since in some cases, it will be the source of the impediments and barriers toward the mobility of the firm within an industry.

Back to the CAS perspective, a system evolves with its environment and as a result of both adaptation and evolution, the new patterns emerge. With reference to the networks, when an organization is embedded within a network, the immediate environment consisting of the relationships of the system is that network through which the system exchanges information and resources, adapts to the changes in the network, or even imposes changes on it albeit it might be minor but, definitely, will impact the context in some ways. Therefore, the study of networks in CAS will not view the relationships merely as relationships, but concurrently viewing them as the environment for an open system. This makes it almost impossible to study the system and its network separately.

Districts

What force the organizations of related industries to accumulate together are the transaction efficiency and flexibility in industrial districts (Malmberg, Solvell, & Zander, 1996). The industrial districts owe their success to the cooperation of their members in innovation and creating knowledge, and product and process innovations were diagnosed as their outcomes (Keeble & Wilkinson, 1998). It is noteworthy that though the innovation might be the outcome, it is not the chief reason behind its formation.

Another type of district which has gained attention and has undergone many changes compared to its initial structure during the recent years is called the innovation districts. They were first designed to be a closed area within specific boundaries aimed at the provision of appropriate environment for innovation (Yigitcanlar, Adu-McVie, & Erol, 2020). Just like what was stated before, the purpose behind the foundation of these districts was merely increasing innovation. Gradually as the environment has continued to change attributable to its dynamic nature, the boundaries have begun to become more and more permeable to the extent that there exist no clear boundaries nowadays, and only blurred boundaries are left. Another change that has happened is the innovation system that has turned into an open innovation system. These districts are of great significance for the nations for the reason that they have become like the economic growth poles for the development in different fields. Their success originates from fostering the formation of networks and collaboration (Yigitcanlar, Adu-McVie, & Erol, 2020), valuing the innovation, and making the environment an innovation-growing place.

The main difference between the innovation districts and the industrial districts are the homogeneity of their structures in respect of the industries their members are active at. While in the innovation districts, firms come from diverse industries, in industrial districts the industry is almost same or at least related. This is ascribed to the difference between the purposes behind their establishment which is innovation for the innovation districts, and for industrial districts are transaction efficiency and flexibility. For instance, companies that work in the telecommunication sector, the medical sector, or even an agricultural sector may be found at a same innovation district for the fact that their common goal is innovation prominently.

Other Agglomerations

The reasons for the preference of agglomerations by the firms are decreasing the spatial distance between the organization and its partners, together with speeding the communication between the suppliers and customers (Malmberg, Solvell, & Zander, 1996). Urban and innovative agglomerations consist of the firms working in different sectors. Urban agglomerations, as perceived from its name, consist of companies located in the same urban area (Boja, 2011).

Like the innovation districts, the purpose of the foundation of innovative agglomerations is innovation while the purposes behind the establishment of urban agglomerations are identical to industrial districts, which are economic efficiency and flexibility.

Bibliography

Ali, S. H. (2015). *Using Complex Adaptive System Theory to Drive System Health Measures for a Province-wide Higher Education System* (Master Thesis ed.). Lethbridge: University of Lethbridge.

Altenburg, T., & Meyer-Stamer, J. (1999). How to Promote Clusters: Policy Experiences from Latin America. *World Development, 27,* 1693–1713.

Anderson, P. (1999). Complexity Theory and Organization Science. *Organization Science, 10*(3), 216–232.

Birkinshaw, J., & Hood, N. (2000). Characteristics of Foreign Subsidiaries in Industry Clusters. *Journal of International Business Studies, 31*(1), 141–154.

Boja, C. (2011). Clusters Models, Factors and Characteristics. *International Journal of Economic Practices and Theories, 1*(1), 34–43.

Carley, K. M. (2005). Intraorganizational Complexity and Computation. In J. A. Baum (Ed.), *The Blackwell Companion to Organizations* (pp. 208–232, Ch 9). Oxford: Blackwell Publishing.

Carlisle, Y., & McMillan, E. (2006). Innovation in Organizations from a Complex Adaptive Systems Perspective. *Emergence: Complexity & Organization, 8*(1), 2–9.

Carpinetti, L. C., Galdamez, E. V., & Gerolamo, M. C. (2008). A Measurement System for Managing Performance of Industrial Clusters; A Conceptual Model and Research Cases. *International Journal of Productivity, 57*(5), 405–419.

Choi, T. Y., Dooley, K. J., & Rungtusanatham, M. (2001). Conceptual Note; Supply Networks and Complex Adaptive Systems: Control versus Emergence. *Journal of Operations Management, 19*, 351–366.

Dayasindhu, N. (2002). Embeddedness, Knowledge Transfer, Industry Clusters and Global Competitiveness: A Case Study of the Indian Software Industry. *Technovation, 22*(9), 551–560.

Dodder, R., & Dare, R. (2000, October 31). *Complex Adaptive Systems and Complexity Theory: Inter-related Knowledge Domains.* Retrieved January 26, 2017, from http://web.mit.edu/esd.83/www/notebook/ComplexityKD.PDF.

Dooley, K. (1996). A Nominal Definition of Complex Adaptive Systems. *The Chaos Network, 8*(1), 2–3.

Dooley, K. J. (1997). A Complex Adaptive Systems Model of Organization Change. *Nonlinear Dynamics, Psychology, and Life Sciences, 1*(1), 69–96.

Eisenhardt, K. M., & Bhatia, M. M. (2005). Organizational Complexity and Computation. In J. A. Baum (Ed.), *The Blackwell Companion to Organizations* (pp. 442–466, Ch 19). Oxford: Blackwell Publishing.

Eisenhardt, K. M., & Sull, D. N. (2001, January). Strategy as Simple Rules. *Harvard Business Review, 79*(1), 107–116.

Fidanboy, M. (2020). *A Multi-level Study of Technoparks within Complex Adaptive Systems Perspective: A Case Study of Factors Influencing R&D Performance* (PhD Dissertation). Ankara: Ankara Yildirim Beyazit University.

Galaskiewicz, J., & Zaheer, A. (1999). Networks of Competitive Advantage. In D. Andrews, & D. Knoke (Eds.), *Research in the Sociology of Organizations* (pp. 237–261). Greenwich, CT: JAI Press.

Gell-Mann, M. (1994). Complex Adaptive Systems. In G. Cowan, D. Pines, & D. Meltzer (Eds.), *Complexity: Metaphors, Models, and Reality* (pp. 17–45). Los Alamos, NM: Addison-Wesley.

George, G., & Lin, Y. (2017). Analytics, Innovation, and Organizational Adaptation. *Innovation: Organization & Management, 19*(1), 16–22.

Gulati, R., Nohria, N., & Zaheer, A. (2000). Strategic Networks. *Strategic Management Journal, 21*(3), 203–215.

Isaksen, A. (1996). *Regional Clusters and Competitiveness: The Norwegian Case.* Oslo, Norway: STEP Group.

Keeble, D., & Wilkinson, F. (1998). Collective Learning and Knowledge Development in the Evolution of Regional Clusters of High Technology SMEs in Europe. *Regional Studies, 33*(4), 295–303.

Malmberg, A., Solvell, Ö., & Zander, I. (1996). Spatial Clustering, Local Accumulation of Knowledge and Firm Competitiveness. *Geografiska Annaler: Series B, Human Geography, 78*(2), 85–97.

Markusen, A. (1996). Sticky Places in Slippery Space: A Typology of Industrial Districts. *Economic Geography, 72*(3), 293–313.

McCarthy, I. P. (2003). Technology Management – A Complex Adaptive Systems Approach. *International Journal of Technology Management, 25*(8), 728–745.

Nan, N. (2011). Capturing Bottom-Up Information Technology Use Processes: A Complex Adaptive Systems Model. *MIS Quarterly, 35*(2), 505–532.

Niu, K.-H. (2010). Industrial Cluster Involvement and Organizational Adaptation: An Empirical Study in International Industrial Clusters. *Competitiveness Review: An International Business Journal, 20*(5), 395–406.

Oughton, E. J., Usher, W., Tyler, P., & Hall, J. W. (2018). Infrastructure as a Complex Adaptive System. *Complexity, 2018*, 1–11.

Porter, M. E. (1990). *The Competitive Advantage of Nations.* New York: Free Press.

Reveiu, A., & Dardala, M. (2012). The Influence of Cluster Type Economic Agglomerations on the Entrepreneurship, in Romania. *Theoretical and Applied Economics, XIX(2012)*, 12(577), 111–124.

Schueler, G. J. (1996, March). The Unpredictability of Complex Systems. *Journal of the Washington Academy of Sciences, 84*(1), 3–12.

Schweitzer, F., Fagiolo, G., Sornette, D., Vega-Redondo, F., & White, D. R. (2009). Economic Networks: What Do We Know and What Do We Need to Know? *Advances in Complex Systems, 12*(4), 1–17.

Siegenfeld, A. F., & Bar-Yam, Y. (2020). An Introduction to Complex Systems Science and Its Applications. *Hindawi, Complexity, 2020*, 1–16.

Stacey, R. D. (1996). *Complexity and Creativity in Organizations* (1st ed.). San Francisco: Berrett Koehler.

Tan, J., Wen, H. J., & Awad, N. (2005, May). Health Care and Services Delivery Systems As complex Adaptive Systems. *Communications of the ACM, 48*, 37–44.

Van Eijnatten, F. M. (2004). Chaos and Complexity: An Overview of the 'New Science' in Organisation and Management. *La Revue des Sciences de Gestion, 40*, 123–165.

Yigitcanlar, T., Adu-McVie, R., & Erol, I. (2020). How Can Contemporary Innovation Districts Be Classified? A Systematic Review of the Literature. *Land Use Policy, Elsevier, 95*(C). DOI: 10.1016/j.landusepol.2020.104595.

2 Complexity

Complexity is used to talk about a great number of different elements (Begun, Zimmerman, & Dooley, 2003; Eidelson, 1997). It was defined as the behavior shown by a CAS which is complicated and is deemed diversely from the complexity noticed in the system itself (Eisenhardt & Bhatia, 2005; Gell-Mann, 1994).

In effect, complexity is the word usually employed in case of encountering problems and issues and is mainly selected to point at the difficulty with respect to the nature of a problem or the difficulty seen in finding the suitable solutions to that problem. A problem will be probably considered complex when it consists of many properties or it is under the impact of numerous factors which makes it to become vaguer, and this increased level of uncertainty is what causes stress and doubt, making the decision makers to go over the same problem and the same solutions time and again, spending extra time and effort on it to finally reach an acceptable solution. Although within each decision, there exists some level of uncertainty, the changing level and the capacity of the decision makers for accepting the uncertainty play roles in labeling a situation as a complex one.

The second condition is when the problem itself does not seem to be complex, but finding the solutions is perceived complex. This usually happens to the decision makers who are prone to view the big picture of the problem, which sometimes results in turning an easily solved problem into a time-taking one. Indeed being able to view the big picture of an issue is an invaluable asset for the decision makers; occasionally, it is not welcomed. In these cases, the complexity of finding solutions is not denied, but there is a need for quick appropriate solutions which can be only reached through simplifying the picture of the problem and acting on it accordingly. The complexity of the solution might be due to the availability of different choices or the absence of a suitable one; selecting from a myriad of solutions may be as hard as finding a feasible solution.

The third probable situation in which a problem is taken complex is the complexity of the context the problem is found at. The complexity of the context may be dependent on various dynamic factors which results in the problem getting complex. This can be clarified via an example.

DOI: 10.4324/9781003182764-2

Suppose a company is planning to purchase a machine from another company in a different country. The decision for purchasing the new machine has been already made, and the need for the new machine had been identified at the first place. In this example, purchasing might not seem to be too complex, and it can be thought as simple as giving the money, and taking the new machine just like the daily shopping an individual does even if the purchased good might be a want instead of a need. In fact, the context of the problem is far more complex than it is seemed at first glance. The questions which can be raised regarding the context may include: Is it a sole manufacturer or are there other manufacturers? Are there any machines produced nationally which can be bought directly instead of importing it? If there is no national manufacturer, then, are the currencies of the two countries same or different? If they are different, in which currency does the transaction take place? How does the taxation change when importing a machine from another country? What are the legal procedures to be followed for the import process? What are the exchange rates? Does the exchange rate change between banks or exchange offices? Is it the right time to exchange money? Will the exchange rate change in the company's favor in the near future? If so, can the purchase be delayed? If the answer is yes, then, how long can it be delayed? If the currencies are same, how will the payment be made? Are there common banks within the two countries? If not, how does the transaction fee change between the banks and what are the preferences for the selection of a bank? These are just some of the questions to be considered for a simple purchase. For those who have been doing a job which involves taking similar decisions constantly, the questions are fixed among the cases, nevertheless, the answers may not show the same consistency over time, and this is the reason why each decision, despite its similarity to the many previous ones, has to be examined carefully each time.

Organizational Complexity

Organizational complexity definitions vary widely, and the operationalization differs accordingly. Organizational size and the structural complexity were mentioned as two of the aspects of organizational complexity (Damanpour, 1996); what is meant by structural complexity may change between studies but it can be summarized as the level of differentiation on diverse dimensions of organizations. Starting from the definition, the traditional approaches toward the complexity were categorized under two main strands: first, the complexity related to the structure of an organization which can be divided into vertical and horizontal complexity, and second, the complexity associated with the behavior of the system (Fioretti & Visser, 2004).

The structural complexity represents the complexity in the elements and their relationships in a system. By complexity, the differentiation of the elements and the number of the elements and the relationships can be signified. The vertical and horizontal division is based on the vertical and horizontal concepts of the structure. The vertical dimension points at the number of hierarchical levels that exist in an organization. For instance, in a software development company the levels can be depicted as the technical team within which there might exist hierarchies as well, the project manager, the chief technology officer, and at the top, the chief executive officer. This may vary between the organizations in different sectors, and even between the organizations from the same sector. Apart from this variety, the hierarchical levels of an organization might change during the lifetime of an organization too; some levels can be added, some can be excluded or interestingly, they can be only labeled differently. For instance, in agile projects, the project manager is sometimes labeled as the scrum master disregarding the righteousness of this action. To sum up, the vertical complexity is the differentiation of the hierarchical levels of an organization compared to its size.

Likewise, the horizontal complexity is the differentiation in the number of units or departments or the job positions at the same level of the hierarchy. In accordance with the purpose of the study, each or some of these dimensions may be chosen to represent the horizontal complexity. For instance, in one of the studies available in the literature, the departmentation and the occupational differentiation were preferred as the dimensions representative of the extent of the horizontal complexity (Damanpour, 1996).

There still remain some gaps which are to be filled with further research concerning the structural complexity. Most of the gaps take their root from the operationalization of the concept, and to be more precise, to turn all these verbal definitions into a number or numbers which can be compared and illustrated much more easily. For those opposing this positivist view, the verbal notion may remain verbal, nonetheless, for the application of agents-based models, and to fulfil the final goal of all these studies, which is running an estimate of the future behavior of the system, there seems to be the need for some kind of quantitative data. What is worth emphasizing here is that the complex adaptive systems are neither predictable nor controllable in a similar vein with what was stated in the literature: the view of the future is unpredictable; one of the assumptions of the complexity science (Fidanboy, 2020; Begun, Zimmerman, & Dooley, 2003). It should be kept in mind that this fact does not devalue the attempts to model the systems and run the simulations and estimations. In some cases, the researchers want to understand the behavior of the system in the past and/or find some explanations for the current behavior of the system. The behavior of the system in future may or may not vary from its previous behavior, it cannot be foreseen, yet, getting to know the system, its elements, the relationships, the patterns of its behavior, all within the boundaries of the system, all out in its environment, and all on its boundaries will provide some ideas on the probable behavior of the system. Even though this is all about probability, even a 1% is worth a lot relative to a mysterious black box where even the elements of the system are not known. Here is where the point rests: managing the complexity. The suggestions and the findings of the studies in complexity science are not after controlling the uncontrollable, nonetheless, managing the complexity has always been of great attention. Managing the complexity is not about controlling. Oppositely, it enables the organization to maintain its freedom between choices of diverse patterns; thus, the organization might be enabled to show these patterns of behavior without being entangled in any impending situations, or being too dependent on the past, deterring it from experiencing the new patterns. Managing the complex adaptive systems is more difficult because these systems are complex and adaptive at the same time. For adaptability to become a lasting property of these systems, the choice between exploration and exploitation must be considered carefully. It is noteworthy that the balance between these two is used for the determination of adaptive capacity of the systems (Duit & Galaz, 2008).

Before looking at the second strand of complexity research, there is a need for clarification. Horizontal and vertical complexity are not the only types of complexity associated with the structure of the organizations. The differentiation may occur in other structural dimensions of the organization as well. The spatial differentiation is another dimension (Daft, Organization Theory and Design, 1992; Anderson, 1999), and the complexity concerned with it originates from the numerous locations at which the employees of a company can work at. To determine the extent of this kind of complexity, factors such as the number of locations, their proximity, and their relationships can be taken into account.

As it is seen, the complexity is mostly taken in association with the structure of the organization, and in many researches, it was defined and measured accordingly. Nevertheless, there were attempts to shift the consideration of complexity as an objective property to the cognitive effort taken by the decision makers for solving the problems and issues the organizations face (Fioretti & Visser, 2004). The second strand of complexity views the complexity as no structural property. In this view, complexity is comprehended as the effects it has on the human cognition specific to each problem or the way the decision makers interpret them (Fioretti & Visser, 2004). In line with the steps taken in this approach, after the preparation of the cognitive map of the decision maker, it is compared with what are seen in practice, and complexity is determined as the extent of their variance. To say it in a straightforward way, the complexity is the mismatch between the reality in the mind and the reality in the real world.

Taking the operationalization, complexity can be measured in accordance with the purpose of the study being taken place. For example, in one study, it was measured as geographic and/or product line diversification, and the industry and geographic concentration were stated as two aspects of the organizational complexity (Bushman, Chen, Engel, & Smith, 2004). In addition, it can be taken as properties of an organization which is associated with the number of parts making up an organization, the diversities among them, and the relationships between them (Fioretti & Visser, 2004).

Like what was mentioned earlier, organizational size is sometimes considered as an aspect of organizational complexity, and sometimes, as an indicator of structural complexity. The measurement of organizational size is usually done using the number of employees in an organization; however, in some studies, the non-personnel indicators were also utilized, for instance, the physical capacity of the organization (Damanpour, 1996). Simply, the organizational size refers to the fact that whether the organization is large or small. When an organization is perceived large, the first reason which comes to the mind is the number of employees. Rethinking about it, then, widen the meaning it implies such as the number of the physical assets or the amount of the resources like financial resources. Precisely, it can denote different meanings as regards the type of the organization. Assuming a hotel as the organization adds an extra meaning to the organizational size. The size of the hotel can be represented as the number of rooms it has. In educational institutions such as schools or universities, the number of students may indicate the organizational size. For a sports facility, the size may be displayed in the form of the number of the branches of sports it provides courses at or, perhaps, the number of its gyms and pools. It doesn't matter which definitions or the indicators for measurement are preferred. The important issue is to select the one consistent with the purpose and the nature of a specific study.

Interorganizational Complexity

Apart from the complexity at the organizational level, it can be present at upper levels as well. Organizations are not isolated properties with no bonds with their context; however, they are sometimes so embedded in their context that makes it hard to identify the boundaries of the organization. This is where the term 'blurred boundaries' is preferred. Beyond the boundaries, whether clear or blurred ones, the other organization, elements, or agents exist which may be in some kind of relationship with the organization. The complexity which is seen between the organizations is dependent on the type of economic agglomeration the organization is posited in. Due to the different characteristics and properties of the numerous economic agglomerations, complexity can be defined for each of them separately.

In clusters, complexity can be identified in relation to the structure of clusters. The factors that influence the degree of complexity in clusters may include the number of firms, the number of dominant firms, the number of firms that are branches of a main firm, the homogeneity of the size of the firms located within the cluster, and the number of connections. In a similar vein with structural complexity in organizations, an increase in the number of the firms, the variety among them, and the number of connections within a cluster are expected to increase the degree of complexity. Conversely, the number of the branches connected to a central firm is anticipated to have a negative relationship since the branches move in harmony with each other which can be considered as a whole; thus, the increase in the number of branches of a certain company in a cluster is predicted to reduce the degree of complexity for that cluster. The homogeneity of the cluster in terms of the sizes of its firms is expected to have a negative relationship with complexity, whereas the increase in the difference between the sizes of the companies is foreseen to increase the complexity. Finally, the more dominant firms can be perceived as more influential decision makers, naturally followed by more decisions and more various types of behavior which raise the cluster complexity.

The complexity of the networks will be much harder to evaluate since networks are more complex with respect to their elements and connections. Within a network, individuals, teams, or organizations can be connected with each other from different geographical locations. Regardless of the type of entities connected, the increase in the number of entities, the rise in the variety of the connections, and the number of various locations are expected to cause the network complexity rise.

Almost true for any other economic agglomerations, the number of the agents and entities, the number of the connections, the variety of the connections, the heterogeneity in terms of the size of the firms in that economic agglomeration, and the number of dominant and controlling firms are proposed to be positively related to the degree of complexity within that economic agglomeration.

Looking back at the literature shows us that the complexity between organizations have attracted more researchers' attention as the partnership and alliances are becoming the popular choices organizations prefer. This need for collaboration and cooperation might root from different reasons. The more dynamic environment compared to the past can be just one of the sources. This way the organization can alleviate the negative outcomes from the risks and the decisions it is taking by sharing it with another partner. This sharing of the bad can be in the form of sharing the monetary loss or even the resources. Imagine the cooperation between two companies. Both companies designate different staff to the common project. It means that they are limiting their human resources for the other projects by this designation or to put it in another way, the employees working on the common project cannot be included in other projects full time. Even if the failure seems to bring no monetary loss to the sides, it sure causes some kind of loss in one or several kinds of the resources since the occupied resources cannot be utilized for the other projects utterly.

Other than sharing the risks taken by collaboration and/or cooperation, the companies can have the resources they haven't had before. These resources might be the ones who bring some kind of competitive advantage. For example, there may be some rare resources owned by a few number of companies, or perhaps, the resource cannot be easily afforded. These can be clarified in the explanation of the cases brought in the following. It might not seem believable when it is presented in the movies; nonetheless, there have always been individuals who are sought out by many companies for working with them. This person may own special technical knowledge, for instance, a great programmer, or may own the experience which makes the companies look for it, like some of the recognized CEOs employed by big companies. When talking of the human resources, one or some of the following three traits may be what makes an individual unique: the knowledge, the skill(s), or the experience. Apart from the human resources, the resource which the company wants to own as a result of the partnership can be a technological asset that is rare or probably costly to afford. Similarly, the nonphysical assets such as a software or a certification or an accreditation can be the reasons behind the partnerships as well. Moreover, the financial resources may push the companies toward the preference of partnership in a similar way. Especially in the small- or medium-sized companies, the realization of some of the goals needs an extra financial resource beyond the companies' affordable financeable resources. In the past, lots of similar cases were seen. To summarize, owning the unaffordable or hard-to afford resources such as human resources and technological resources can tempt the companies into partnerships.

Bibliography

Anderson, P. (1999). Complexity Theory and Organization Science. *Organization Science, 10*(3), 216–232.

Begun, J. W., Zimmerman, B., & Dooley, K. (2003). Health Care Organizations as Complex Adaptive Systems. In S. M. Mick, & M. Wyttenbach (Eds.), *Advances in Health Care Organization Theory* (pp. 253–288). San Francisco: Jossey-Bass.

Bushman, R., Chen, Q., Engel, E., & Smith, A. (2004). Financial Accounting Information, Organizational Complexity and Corporate Governance Systems. *Journal of Accounting and Economics, 37*(2), 167–201.

Daft, R. L. (1992). *Organization Theory and Design* (4th ed.). St Paul, MN: West.

Damanpour, F. (1996). Organizational Complexity and Innovation: Developing and Testing Multiple Contingency Models. *Management Science, 42*(5), 693–716.

Duit, A., & Galaz, V. (2008). Governance and Complexity – Emerging Issues for Governance Theory. *Governance: An International Journal of Policy, Administration, and Institutions, 21*(3), 311–335.

Eidelson, R. J. (1997). Complex Adaptive Systems in the Behavioral and Social Sciences. *Review of General Psychology, 1*(1), 42–71.

Eisenhardt, K. M., & Bhatia, M. M. (2005). Organizational Complexity and Computation. In J. A. Baum (Ed.), *The Blackwell Companion to Organizations* (pp. 442–466, Ch 19). Oxford: Blackwell Publishing.

Fidanboy, M. (2020). *A Multi-level Study of Technoparks within Complex Adaptive Systems Perspective: A Case Study of Factors Influencing R&D Performance* (PhD Dissertation). Ankara: Ankara Yildirim Beyazit University.

Fioretti, G., & Visser, B. (2004). A Cognitive Approach to Organizational Complexity. *Tinbergen Institute Discussion Paper, No. 04-033/1, Tinbergen Institute, Amsterdam and Rotterdam*, 1–32.

Gell-Mann, M. (1994). *Complex Adaptive Systems.* Retrieved January 26, 2017, from http://tuvalu.santafe.edu/~mgm/Site/Publications_files/MGM%2011 3.pdf.

3 Adaptation

Adaptation is one of the many concepts which can be investigated at numerous levels. The adaptation at the microlevel of a society is the individual adaptation. Scales were developed to measure the individual adaptation, and they are used for various purposes such as recruitment or directing the candidates toward the fields of study they are mostly fitted with characteristically. The individuals' adaptive capacities differ just like many other personality traits. Some accept the changes sooner and easier than the others and then show adaptive responses. These adaptive responses can be in different forms. They may take actions in order to conform to the changes or conversely, their actions are in the direction of decreasing the changes or the possible effects of the changes. The other group of individuals are the ones who don't want to accept the changes and want to keep on with their old behavior. This is the situation at which the inertia occurs. The organizational inertia is a known phenomenon and there are myriads of research about it, yet before being considered as an organizational notion, it originates from the behavior of the individuals in an organization. As it is comprehended, one main issue with multilevel concepts is that how these concepts are related to each other at different levels. To be more precise and clear, if the adaptation of the individuals working at the department of an organization is measured, and, at the same time, the adaptation of their department is identified by measurement as well, how their relationship impacts on one another can be explained. There are many questions to seek answers for: Are there any formulas or a set of processes through which the individual adaptation measurements can be then turned into one upper level measurement, for example, the adaptation of their department? How are these different level concepts related and how do they affect each other? How is a change in one of them reflected in the other one's amount? What are the factors influencing each of them and both of them? The answers to all of these questions and other similar questions provoke a final question present at the end of every research which is whether the findings can be generalized or not. Even if a research embraces all the answers, the issue is in which context the research has been conducted and how similar is this context to the other contexts so that the same findings can be reached. The

DOI: 10.4324/9781003182764-3

generalization is what makes it hard to spread the findings to any other contexts.

One of the very famous issues concerning the adaptation is the dialectical debate of adaptation and selection. While some scientists view them as two opposite notions, some others think of them as a complementary notion, yet the third view of them in the character of two interrelated processes of change (Levinthal, 1991) is more close to the approach of this book. The first critique to the preference of this approach originates from the use of the word 'adaptive' in the CAS perspective; therefore, it is automatically perceived that the approach of CAS toward the debate is in favor of adaptation. The organizational inertia plays the principal role in their relation. Organizational inertia was suggested as the basis for selection and the inertial forces in the role of a prerequisite for intelligent organizational adaptation (Levinthal, 1991). The following explanations can help with the clarification of this paradoxical role. Imagine an organization that has detected changes in its environment. It is making preparations to take actions toward gaining a new fit with it like many other rivals in the same environment. Some of the organizations will act more rapidly compared to others. In biology, when talking of selection, the populations of animals or plants are examined for several generations during an almost long period of time. There, the duration of the study seems to be more crucial than the speed the dominant group consumes the resources in the environment. The speed is also of great momentousness for the reason that the environmental resources are constrained, and they can be hardly available to everyone, and the one who is faster can take advantage of the resources. If the advantage is the food, the latecomers may lose their chance for survival, and through this, the selection eventuates. In a similar vein with biology, in the organizational studies, the same rules are valid. The companies delayed for the adaptation to their environment bear the least or no probability to survive in spite of the fact that the failure or the vanishing of the company may take some time like the examples in biology. In biology, many factors determine whom to survive, whom and when to become extinct, such as the type of the resource in the environment, or the scarcity and vitality of that resource for that specific population. Considering it from the resource dependency theory of the organizations, the resources and their changes can trigger the adaptation process in the organizations as well. Suppose there is only one manufacturer for a hardware used in a widely used electric device. All the manufacturers of that electric device are highly dependent on their supplier, part of their environment. The hardware manufacturer is moving on to altering the hardware with a new version which will not be compliant with old electric devices. Here, the speed matters. The electric device manufacturers have to make their manufacturing processes consistent with the new hardware, otherwise, they will face the problem of supplying the old hardware, and they have to stop their production. The electric device manufacturer who changes its production line accordingly can conquer the market for a period of time till the other rivals adapt too.

The rivals might go under the required changes or might fail. Granted all mentioned, the significance of the speed in providing the appropriate adaptive response can be neither denied nor underrated. This also implies that the selection can be done based on the organizational inertia. Besides, the inertia enhances the efficacy of selection in the organizations (Levinthal & Marin, 2015).

This is now the turn to elucidate the relationship between the adaptation and the inertial forces. Notwithstanding the drawbacks of inertia and the problems it causes, it can be advantageous in some cases. With reference to the example of the electric device manufacturer, another scenario can be devised. Among the electric device manufacturers, one adapted faster than the others and had lots of sales. The other manufacturers joined him too after a few months. As time passed, users started to complain about the new version of the electric device, a problem which was related to the use of the new hardware. All the electric device manufacturers contacted their seldom supplier to ask for returning to the old hardware. Hence, the hardware manufacturer began producing the new versions of the same old hardware, and the only electric device manufacturer who had the appropriate production line left for the old hardware was the delayed one in adaptation, the one with the highest organizational inertia. This can be considered as a kind of intelligent adaptation roots from the inertial forces. The very similar example can be the companies active in very turbulent environments such as the stock market. The delays generated by the inertial forces bring more time to the company for making more logical and wiser decisions which lead to earning more profits from time to time.

Organizational Adaptation

An organization as a whole bear many characteristics, and they have always been the interests of the researchers. The organization may be hard to be supposed as a living thing; however, as long as it lives it shows certain types of behavior and holds specific characteristics. Just like the personal traits at the individual level, each organization possesses some features and characteristics which make it identifiable from other organizations such as age, size, identity, and so on.

One of the very interesting studies was the one exploring diverse perspectives toward organizational adaptation. In that study, some of the main organizational theories were categorized under three main perspectives: deterministic, voluntaristic, and coevolutionary (Abatecola, 2012). As comprehended from their names, the deterministic perspectives include the theories which consider the environment as the key role for selecting which organizations can survive; thus, the fate of an organization is determined by the environment. In contract, the voluntaristic views highlight the role of the management in taking actions on the environment voluntarily; therefore, they have the chance to select their responses. With reference to the coevolutionary perspectives, the first two perspectives can exist at different periods of time and at different intensities (Abatecola, 2012).

The studies on organizational adaptation were suggested to regard three groups of variables: the variables associated with the environment, the variables related to the structure of the organization, and strategy making (Miller & Friesen, 1980). The debate between the structure and the strategy gains attention in this condition; whether the strategy comes before the structure or the structure is prior to the strategy. Using the CAS perspective, the change in the structure means any kind of changes in the elements of the systems or their connections while the change in strategy originates from the changes in the behavior shown by the agents, and this behavior itself originates from the schemata of the actors or decision makers. Consistent with the changes infused into the system, there may be a need to modify the schemata or change the structure of the system. To be plainer, the CAS perspective does not make any specific preference between strategy and structure, but leave the choice to be made in consistency with the situation. This is when adaptation makes sense.

Adaptation to the environment depends on many factors. The factors can be grouped as environmental factors and organizational factors if to be viewed as an open system from a CAS perspective. In line with the assumptions held for the open systems, these systems have boundaries that separate the systems from their environment. This categorization of the factors will be the easiest way to investigate them. Starting with the organizational factors, there will be many of them like the employees' openness to change, their individual adaptive capacity, the structure of the organization in terms of its flexibility to adapt, and the decision makers as the key roles. In most of the researches, the organizational construct comes forward, and the role of the decision makers in the adaptation is usually faded and dissolved when exploring the construct at the organizational level. Nonetheless, the decision makers influence the adaptation in countless ways. In the available literature on the organizational adaptation, the importance of how decision makers interpret their environment was emphasized (Ford & Baucus, 1987), and these are the interpretations on which the organizations act in response to the changes. The other possible way of the decision maker's influence is how he depicts the changes in the eyes of the other employees. If he does not welcome changes, the chance that employees will welcome the changes will be low. For example, a manager is introducing some new requirements as part of the adaptive response, but he uses the words which can be perceived in a negative way. In such a situation, when the employees don't feel the support from the top management, they may not accept the changes or they may not be fully committed to them. One of the factors which impact the acceptance of the changes may be the job satisfaction of the employees. The employees unsatisfied with their jobs may be more unwilling to endure any changes when the changes seem to be hard to be implemented. Another factor can be the organizational commitment. Regardless of the kind of the commitment, the less commitment might be related to less contribution to the adaptation processes.

Looking at the structure of the organizations, determination of the type best for being adaptive is not that easy. The structure of an organization has many dimensions such as formalization, specialization, and centralization (Daft, 2007). There will be a host of combinations of all these dimensions and each will show a different level of adaptation when confronting changes. This requires further research to predict the adaptation of these combinations in different contexts. In part of the literature, the companies with high R&D performance were found to show more adaptation in all the dimensions except for rules and regulations when compared with the companies with low R&D performance (Fidanboy, 2020).

Adaptive responses have been brought up a lot in all previous discussions, but what is really meant by adaptive responses needs some more explanations and examples. Suppose you are the manager of a food company. The manufacturing processes are done on a regular basis and everything seems to be monotonously going on. Even you, as the manager, sign the same papers and do the same office work. Do you think everything will keep working like this forever? Of course, not. Even in the bluest ocean, when no competitors are present and no one seems to enter the market for a long time, what you view as a slight and minor change can ruin all the routines, procedures, and processes. All at once, a new scientific research shed light on the potential harms on one of the ingredients in your products, and the media begin making news of these harmful ingredients. The sale starts to fall drastically. What happened to that blue ocean? You have no choice except finding solutions or downsizing your company which will continue till the complete collapse of the company and failure of your strategies as a manager. Your employees will start to blame you as the manager for not being able to predict such an incident or at least finding a solution when it happens. Referring to the scientific terminology, the first response is called the proactive response and the latter response is the reactive response to the changes. In the similar vein with the literature, adaptation is not all waiting for the changes in the environment to occur and then initiating the reactions accordingly (Cameron, 1984). It is worth emphasizing that the proactive responses are also demonstrated in the existence of some kind of mismatch between the organization and the environment. It cannot be necessarily a change in the environment, but a change inside the organization which gives rise to an inconsistency between the organization and the environment it is posited at. The point which should be paid attention to is that what is labelled as the adaptation is any kind of changes sourcing from the environment or imposed on the organization by the environment even if the changes seemed to root from something within the organization at the first glance. As the managers, the identification of the main sources of changes requires more than taking a look at it, but deepening the understanding of the change and the factors affecting it, and finally, pinpointing the source.

In addition to the reactive and proactive responses to the changes in the environments, there is another possible situation in terms of the relationship between the environment and the organization which was named as 'defensive' (Chakravarthy, 1982). The companies that are 'defenders' (Chakravarthy, 1982) try to ignore the changes in the environment, and in spite of making adjustments, they make efforts to narrow their exchange with their environment and deter from interacting with it. The decisions are then made and the strategies are defined according to this approach. The success of such companies is dependent on the level of similarity between the future and today's environment. If the environment stays same as before, they have the opportunity to survive, though today's dynamic environment aggravates the possibility of success and survival.

Two main reasons were provided for the selection of specific adaptive responses by the firms which are the adaptive ability consisting of organizational and material capacity along with the process of adaptation which embraces adaptive generalization and adaptive specialization (Chakravarthy, 1982). This categorization can be further expanded to the debate between the strategy and structure. During the adaptive generalization, the adjustments in the material and organizational capacity are followed by the adjustments in the strategy while at the time of the adaptive specialization process, the modifications and alterations in the strategy induce the structure of the organization to adapt accordingly.

One of the very enlightening explanations was exhibited in the literature on how to differentiate planned change from adaptation. To summarize, some of the main differences of planned organizational change and the adaptation were proffered as the source of the changes, the level of the changes whether individual or organizational, the focus of change, and their literature (Cameron, 1984). These can be described with some examples from the practice and experience. Moving back to the food company example, the change related to the ingredients is compelled to the company from the environment; hence, this is considered an adaptation. In the same company, training is scheduled for the employees in the manufacturing process in association with a food standard. The training is supposed to be informative and educative in a supplementary way as the employees have already known the standard. The management decides to hire a consultant to assure that what had been taught during the training are executed in practice as well. After several weeks, some behavioral changes in the employees are seen in accordance with the training concepts. Some visible changes are like being more careful, more cautious, and performing more elaborate observations. Having it viewed from the eye of an organizational researcher, the training has obviously impacted the organizational culture. Approaching from a CAS perspective, the changes in the schemata of the employees have resulted the changes in their behaviors and these changes are also be reflected in the organizational culture. This type of organizational change is not taken into account as an adaptation but as a planned organizational change. As it has always been of great attention, in uncertain and dynamic environments, the adaptation matters more, when predications and anticipations can hardly be made or require professional insight and knowledge.

The next difference between the planned organizational change and adaptation is the focus of change which are intraorganization and on the exchange of resources and information between the organization and its environment, respectively. The last difference is their literature. For the planned organizational changes, the manager or the project manager or the one has the authority prepares a plan containing cost, budget, and time needed for the change along with the scope of the change. In some of the companies, there are forms required to be filled out for the approved changes. On the other hand, the literature of adaptation is about how the changes are taking place and what is obtained from the adaptation at the end. Like what mentioned earlier, the adaptation is a process, not a rule, not a specific task or a product. It is more about answering the 'how' questions rather than the 'what' questions.

Another issue related to the adaptation is the modes of adaptation; what the different kinds of adaptation are, to say it simply. In this respect, 'track' was introduced as the paths taken by the organization over its lifecycle, and it can be used to explain whether the organization will change and if so, how it will change (Fox-Wolfgramm, Boal, & Hunt, 1998). In the same article, four different modes for adaptation were discussed. Integrating these modes of adaptation with the assumptions of CAS produces the following four possible conditions a system may experience at the time of encountering with changes. Before moving through the conditions, emergence should be discussed first. What is implied by emergence is the new patterns, properties, qualities, or structures that appear in the system (Mitleton-Kelly, 2003) as a result of change. As for the first condition, facing some of the changes leads to the emergence temporarily, and after some time, the organization will go back to its initial status. It cannot be a good example in terms of the nonethical issues it bears; however, it is just like the organizations under some kind of appraisal, and during the time of their appraisal, they make some changes. After the appraisal is finished, they start doing what they do as they did before and everything goes back to its previous form.

The second condition is the permanent emergence. The organization takes a new form in terms of one, all or some of the patterns of behaviors, properties, the structures, or/and qualities. For instance, a new model is going to be applied to an organization for the purpose of improving some of the current processes, creating some new processes, and excluding some of them. The organization will keep on doing the processes in their updated manner. One example of this condition can be a transition from using the traditional project management to agile methods. In such a case, not only the processes are modified and altered, but also some structural modifications will be made. The traditional project management is compliant with the hierarchical structure of the organizations, whereas the agile methods favor and suggest a more vertical structure. Till now, in this example, the processes and the structure have been changed. Moving forward with the same example, the agile methods welcome changes while the traditional project management is more reluctant to infuse any changes into the project after the planning. This is reflected in the difference between their quality approaches, the customer-oriented quality approach, and the outcome–income-based quality approach, respectively. As a result, in this case, the emergence of new patterns of behaviors is demonstrated too. The emergence of new patterns of behavior can also be noticed as a result of the change in the hierarchical structure. In the traditional project management, the project manager is the authority control who checks and orders the members of the technical team; nonetheless, in the agile methods, the hierarchy is not seen, and the one standing near the team, helping them, and guiding them is called coach or master based on the agile method being utilized. This omission of the command-control authority induces behavioral changes in the members of the team like feeling more motivated to work, more willing to share their new ideas, more creative, or more helpful to their team members. Granted all mentioned, the agile methods are one group of methods very well fitted within the CAS perspective as they are concentrated on the acceptance of changes throughout the project lifecycle. This implicitly points toward the constant adaptation since the source of the changes is mostly customers, beyond the boundaries of the organization, part of its environment.

The third condition is chaos. Imagine an axis. On the left side is the order state, in the middle is the complexity, and on the right side rests the chaos state ranging from zero connections to full connections (Potts, 2000). In the chaos condition, the system experiences no dominant pattern, but fluctuating between different patterns. The absence of a structure makes barriers on the way of the exchange of information which, at last, will cause the system to 'disintegrate into unpredictable performance' (Comfort, 1994). What is needed to be stressed here is that creativity and innovation come about at the edge of chaos (Bak, 1996; Faucher, 2010).

The fourth condition is what was labelled as inertia (Fox-Wolfgramm, Boal, & Hunt, 1998). It happens when the organization resists the change and it is reluctant to experience any kind of changes, trying to maintain its previous pattern. The inertia is one of the key issues at the failure of the change. Poor change management cannot handle the inertia naturally shown by the organization. The use of the word 'naturally' is to accentuate the fact that inertia, as originated from natural sciences, is accompanied with natural phenomena. It is not a notion that exist apart and then added to the phenomena, but it comes with them in a natural manner. Inertia may seem to be a trivial matter, yet it has been among the main reasons the organization couldn't implement the change desirably. Taking a look at one real-world example can shed light on this fact. An educational organization tended to apply a new system to its language-teaching processes. The employees were designated for each of the tasks planned to get done.

For the aim of control and check, a person was assigned the tasks related to supervision. After a few months, the outcomes of the system were not as expected. From an organizational studies viewpoint, the organization's attempts for executing the changes might not be sufficient or appropriate. Sometimes the team members do not attempt enough to achieve the goals or oppositely, they make lots of efforts but the efforts are not made in the right direction for reaching the goal. The continuous effort with no desired outcome gained is just one of the factors that make the employees to become worn out and in some cases, it eventually ends with quitting. The same thing happened in this instance. After several months, the turnover rate increased and even those who didn't leave their jobs have thought of resignation at least once. What was not foreseen in this case was the inertia on the way to change. In agreement with what was stated before, the inertia cannot be prevented, but can be mitigated to the level which does the least harm to the organization, to the extent it would not be felt much. Managers, based on their knowledge or experience, have diverse ways to deal with inertia. For the example discussed earlier, inertia could have been mitigated by more transparency in terms of giving description on the tasks, the process of the assignments of the tasks, the benefits provided by the changes, and the justifications for the need for the changes. This may not suffice without a control mechanism. The tasks should be observed closely, and the staff should be monitored constantly to see whether they are performing according to the plans or not. Too much observation and monitoring may have negative effects on the employees. A useful solution can be self-organized teams in which the team members are empowered to add their own methods and techniques, and they are kept motivated to work, committed to the changes. What should be kept in mind is that even the strictest model or framework devised for implementation in the organizations presents the option of tailoring. Not every change is absolutely profitable for every organization or every context. Consequently, a good decision is to leave some subjects open to negotiations through a small and trivial amount, so that the employees feel the empowerment and the value organization gives them. Being able to speak their opinions and ideas openly can help to increase their motivation and job satisfaction, and the feeling of being actively involved in the process of change makes them more committed. Commitment to the changes is very crucial throughout the change period as it may vary easily due to many factors. Keeping the members of the organizations committed is one of the responsibilities of the managers. There are many companies which are really hard for people to get into, and those who start working in these companies usually won't resign, but continue working till their retirement. Whatever their commitment strategy is, they are successful in preventing the drawbacks originating from the turnover, especially the turnover of human resources which are the source of competitive advantages.

A very similar and almost same concept to adaptation modes were named as the adaptation forms: relative inertia, adjustment, reorientation, and strategic renewal (Burgelman, 1991). These forms were defined and described in association with the strategy-making processes. Here, they are integrated with CAS perspective, explained within examples. An electronics company has just changed its R&D strategies to catch up with the worldwide technological innovations. The R&D strategy changes were imposed on the company as a result of their choice for entering the global market. Viewing it from a CAS lens illustrates the widening of the environment; the national market remains while an international market has been added. The part of the environment new to the organization urges it to take new steps toward reaching a fit with the bigger environment. Consequently, the strategies were modified. After some time, the fit turns into the misfit for the reason that the requirements for the fit have been replaced, and the environmental changes trigger more strategic changes in the organizations posited within it. What is simply needed is to change the strategies again. The new changes can also take place, nevertheless, the relativity of inertia points at the reduction of such changes as time passes, and when making a comparison between the changes required by the environment and the changes in the strategies, the changes in the strategies will be relatively lower. The reactive response is the most probable response at the first stages of the process, even so, by the time passing, reactive responses are less made and thus, the defensive responses will become perceptible.

The adjustment argument delineates that despite the inertia on the way to adaptation, adjustments, even minor ones, may come out. Although the minor adjustments are useful to some point, after a period, there are needs for major changes of the strategies. The aforementioned electronics company might go on with some minor changes, yet the strategies will not be fruitful, sufficient, and legitimate later. This is consistent with the earlier discussions of temporary emergence and permanent emergence. The emergence of new strategies can be temporarily experienced, but the permanent emergence will be demanded eventually. In terms of the type of response, the reactive response is seen during adjustment.

The reorientation is same as the chaos state described earlier. The interesting issue here is that the major changes in the strategies might save the organization from the collapse for the time being, albeit in the long term, it decreases the life expectancy of the organization (Burgelman, 1991). In addition, the type of adaptive response is mainly reactive, waiting for the environment to force changes on the organization and then commencing taking actions. Regarding the electronic company, the company efforts in order to develop its R&D activities had continued, even though, due to the major changes in the structure pursued by major changes in the strategy, it had already made lots of trouble for the company. The strategies worked at first; nonetheless, after several months of struggling, the company failed in the global market and receded to its previously concentrated national market. It is noteworthy that the concept of environment for a CAS as a kind of open system might be deemed more related to natural sciences than the social studies, although underestimating it in the social studies will give rise to devastating problems and failures to the organizations. Consequently, before making any decisions concerning the environment like expanding the environment by entering into new markets, or changing the environment by changing the product manufactured, or the service being provided, or changing the location of the company, the changes which were and are in demand by the environment should be explored well. The current needs should not suffice for a deep comprehensive understanding of the environment; thus, it would be better to take a look back at the history of the environment and investigate the trend of the changes in the past, probing into the factors playing key roles in the changes, and further, link the past with the current situation. The lack of a clear view of the environment is a barrier on the adaptation processes since the environment is what the organization intends to adapt to.

The last adaptation mode is the strategic renewal. During the strategic renewals, first, the internal experimentation and selection occur which are what differentiate the renewal from reorientation, followed by strategic changes which helps the organization to remain adaptive (Burgelman, 1991). Moreover, the strategic renewal enables the company to show proactive adaptive responses in the future (Burgelman, 1991).

The adaptation modes have been discussed earlier in this section. A question which is still left unanswered is that 'what makes the organizations choose similar or different adaptation modes?' Three sources of forces were offered for the similarities between the choices of the adaptation modes: coercive, normative, and mimetic forces – where coercive forces compel the organizations to select the same modes while the normative forces root from the norms regarding the institutional context, and the mimetic forces are related to the imitation of the mode preferred by the successful organizations (Fox-Wolfgramm, Boal, & Hunt, 1998).

The extent to which organizations experience adaptation differ, and a division was made in the literature for the levels. According to an article, an organization can go under the adaptation at different levels: high, medium, and low levels (Jennings & Seaman, 1994). The relationship between the adaptation and the structure of the companies has become apparent in the same study. The structure of the firm is either as organic or as mechanistic structure, where the organic structure has the flexibility to adapt to the changes compared to the mechanistic structure which is more rigid and stricter toward the changes. In this regard, the organizations with high level of adaptation will have organic structure, whereas the organizations with adaptation of low level will have mechanistic structure (Jennings & Seaman, 1994). One good example of the companies with organic structure is the companies that are implementing agile frameworks. Such companies do not possess the traditional hierarchical structure through which the communication whenever needed should follow the below-top or the top-below directions. The communication is so frequent in these companies and it is mostly taking place among the vertical levels. Whenever communication between hierarchical levels is required, due to the low number of levels, it can also occur quickly and easily comparatively.

With regard to the rules, the companies with organic structure are mainly working with fewer but just fundamental rules, whereas in the companies with mechanistic structure, conformance to the rules is of great importance to the point that it sometimes turns into chains, keeping the organizations from finding an optimal solution rapidly, and it costs time to the organization, besides, in some situations it is accompanied by the negligence of creative and innovative solutions. Furthermore, adaptation in terms of rules and regulation has shown a different behavior from other dimensions of adaptation among companies with low and high R&D performance. The high performers were found to show more adaptation in terms of all organizational adaption dimensions except for rules and regulations (Fidanboy, 2020). The occurrence of adaptation in dimension may be low due to the few numbers of rules and regulations in high performers. They don't feel any need to modify or alter these few rules for two main reasons; the first is that they are few in number, and the second reason is that the rules are the fundamental rules, rarely demanded to be altered.

Moving toward the field of practice, one of the very useful features of the agile companies is the omission of the extra unnecessary hierarchical levels which brings about numerous critical benefits. First, the communication taken place at the vertical level can be done in a shorter time, and subsequently, the solutions can be reached faster. Second, the employees may feel more empowered, less under pressure and stressed when the hierarchical structure does not compel them to report their works to the upper levels, but to a person at the same level with them, designated as the team coach or the team master. Third, whenever new ideas and opinions emerge at the technical level, they should not follow all the hierarchical levels since they will be reported directly to the coach at the same level. The convenience provided to the employees for sharing their thoughts and ideas makes the working environment more innovative and creative. In spite of efficiency, the effectiveness of the agile methods cannot be denied. Fourth, in the agile organizations, the changes are proceeded neither in a top-down manner nor in a down-top manner, however, within and through the organization as a whole. The approval of the changes will usually need the confirmation from the top management or any other top-level authority; hence, they will be informed of the changes. Nonetheless, the changes do not go through all top-down structures to be announced to the technical team members. Conversely, the approved changes are handled by the team coach or master and shared with the technical team members directly. This is the prominent reason why the agile organization are good at adaptation, dissolving the change right into the project.

'Which organizations are successful in terms of adaptation?' has been the main research question of many studies. Some of the characteristics for the organizations with successful adaptation are: having flexible structure, going under more changes, recruiting employees more than removing them from their jobs, bearing a higher ratio of change to the number of agents (Carley, 1997). The changes in an organization come out at two levels: strategic and operational levels (Carley, 1997). At the strategic level, an organization make attempts to obtain a fit with its environment through the strategies being made while the operational level adaptation is about the agents performing the tasks in the organizations and are capable of learning from the experience and using the lessons learnt in their future execution of tasks. The learning is a crucial characteristic sought in the employees in adaptive organizations. Considering the agile companies as a good exemplification of the adaptive organizations, the learning takes place throughout the project, all the time. It is happening continuously and the lessons learnt are both stored in the memories of the team members along with keeping them in written forms, either hard or soft forms as a guide for future reference. The advantage of agile companies with respect to the lessons learnt is that they don't leave the learning to the employees due to the fact that the lessons learnt might be perceived dissimilarly from one individual to another one and may be forgotten after some time. Thus, after the completion of a project, the team members and other authorities gather in a meeting to discuss the lessons they have learnt from the completed project and they are recorded and saved for further reference. Since the agile companies confront the changes a lot, they should be so careful with their decisions in order to make wise and appropriate decisions, together with making efforts to avoid the past mistakes.

In a similar vein with the levels of changes in an organization, the capability of learning can be investigated at two levels in an organization as well: the strategic and the operational level (Carley & Lee, 1998). At the strategic level, the learning is done by altering the connections, whereas at the operational level, the employees obtain experience (Carley & Lee, 1998).

A model consisting of five processes was proposed for the organizational adaptation to environmental changes: scanning, noticing, interpretation, choosing, and learning (Milliken, Dutton, & Beyer, 1992). These processes will be explained integrated with the CAS perspective. Consider an electronics company which produces home appliances. Employees in almost all departments related to the production usually research for the new technologies, changes in the market, changes in the needs of customers, follow the latest trends related to home appliances, and a host of other information. Of course, not all the information is useful and can be utilized later. Thus, some of the information is worth paying attention to since the attentional resources were stated to be constrained (Milliken, Dutton, & Beyer, 1992). The next stage is to interpret the data which were noticed before. The interpretation is a subjective process just like the noticing process for the reason that what data should be heeded and what should be omitted is dependent on the subjectivist view of the relevant agents together with how to interpret the data. These subjectivist opinions and decisions remind the cognitive part of a CAS, schemata. The schemata, the source of the behavior shown by the individuals, bear an important role especially during these two processes. What is labelled as the organizational schemata will help to reduce the disagreements and variations among diverse interpretations; nonetheless, in case of any existing disagreements which cannot be fixed or when sufficient information is not supplied for making the right interpretation, a scanning process will be asked to be repeated. Subsequently, the noticing process will face some changes too. This feedback mechanism assures the decision makers to make the most intelligent decision despite all uncertainty that is present in all projects all the time. What matters here is that the uncertainty that is not inevitable in any projects can be thought of, which implies the uncertainty of the environment. On the other hand, the organization is a CAS and its behavior is neither predictable nor controllable. Thus, good managers don't tend to control the behavior of a CAS or predict it as it is not really feasible. A good decision is the one being made after taking into consideration all available data as well as exploring the history of the organization including, but not limited to, the best practices, experiences, lessons learnt, and the previous decisions.

The next process of organizational adaptation is choosing the best interpretation of the problems and changes which will be then responded to. The selection of the interpretation is again partially subjective. The data based on the fact shape the objective part of the decision; nonetheless, due to the involvement of a decision-making process or to be clearer, the engagement of the cognitive map of the decision makers with the decision making is partly subjective too. This is true for almost every matter dealt with in management. In spite of the use of engineering tools and other quantitative tools in the field of management and the organizational studies, these tools remain solely as supportive tools, not determining tools. The data are given to the software or are entered into the processing and the information is the outcome either in a qualitative form or in a quantitative form. Based on this information and the experience and knowledge of the decision maker, a decision is made. The quantitative information such as the tables depicting the production on a monthly basis cannot be reported to the employees labeled as the 'new decision of the manager.' These raw information needs to be processed cognitively to become comprehensible and executable. The decisions are next announced in the form of statements or in some cases, they may include a quantitative statement like increasing the production by 10% which is the outcome of processing the information extracted from software, figures, tables, etc., subsequently simplified in such a sentence to be clearly understood by the relevant staff. The clarity of the decisions is an important issue which its dearth causes many problems. Some examples associated with the vagueness attributable to the use of words when numbers are needed are 'increase in production is needed' or 'the deadline is next month.' The questions rise after such statements are: 'How much increase is aimed at? How is the increase calculated; in the form of percentage or the number of products manufactured?' or 'when is exactly the deadline? Which day? What is the date?' To conclude, the management of an organization is involved with both objective and subjective decisions and, additionally, dealing with quantitative and qualitative data and information.

Learning is the last process of organizational adaptation, through which the organization begins taking actions in response to the changes in the environments. The first issue here is that the organization must learn how to learn. Furthermore, the culture of the organization should support the learning as well. The trainings, workshops, and seminars organized by the organizations for their employees are just some of the means for reaching this goal. Giving promotion to the employees who continue learning new skills is another way to buoy the learning culture in the organization.

Interorganizational Adaptation

The organizations in a network may be loosely or tightly connected with each other. As the strength of the connections varies, the characteristics of the connections differ too. In one of the previous studies, the findings suggested that strong ties help the organizations to reduce the uncertainty and foster adaptation through communication and sharing information with others (Kraatz, 1998). Thus, it can be implied that the weak relationships would not assist the organization in dealing with the changes in the environment. The exchange of information is not good in weak relationships, and the organization may not receive enough information regarding the changes in the environment or concerning the actions the other organizations are taking in response to the changes toward the adaptation.

Apart from the strength of the connections within a network, the size of the network also plays an important role in predicting the benefits it provides its members with or, oppositely, the restrictions it chains its organizations with. What is usually seen in the organization with large networks is that they have the novel information sooner than the atomistic organizations, and thus, whenever being fast is required in this dynamic world, they are the ones who exceed their rivals in this rat race. Such a situation may not always be of advantage. The risk of the diffusion of wrong information, which is sometimes spread to trap the organizations, is so high. This not-on-fact-based information are created by the organizations to cause harm to the others, and make them involved in a situation, distracting them from what is actually going on and making them waste their resources on unnecessary issues. It is the responsibility of the decision makers to be wise in detecting the truthfulness of information and then start acting on them. The other problem with the large networks is that the communication may not be as frequent as in the small networks along with the less intimacy. For instance, an organization located in a large network can have close and frequent relationships with several organizations, but not the rest. To say it more clearly, the frequency and the closeness of the connections of an organization is not necessarily the same through all of its connections.

Looking at the adaptation in large networks, the organizations have the chance to gain more information from more resources, be aware of their environment more, and therefore, showing more suitable adaptive responses. On the other hand, in networks of small size, the information resources might not be that many, though they have the chance to observe the organizations closely, watch their actions, copy their adaptive actions, or tailor them based on their needs or even deterring the wrong adaptive responses to be given by the organization. Both large and small networks provide some advantages and disadvantages to their members in terms of adaptation. Nevertheless, it is noteworthy that the size and the strength of connections are not the only factors with influence on the adaptation responses in a network.

Till now, some of the characteristics of the connections have been mentioned; the frequency and the length. By length, the closeness is meant; an arm-length connection represents a close relationship between the organizations. The third characteristic is the age of the connection, whether the connection has been recently established or it is old enough to bring what the passing of time brings to the relationships. The effect of time in the relationship is not negligible; the actors know each other well and they can predict each other's future actions. In its positive manner, mutual trust can be formed while in the negative manner, it restricts the choices of organization in terms of the options to work with. From a CAS point of view, the aforementioned possible cases are related to path dependency in making decisions concerning the partners and collaborators. Not too high or too low level of path dependency is desired but an average level. Taken all said so far, the strength of the connection is dependent on the frequency, length, and the age of the connection.

The fourth characteristic, which is a determinant of the strength of the connection, is whether there is an amplifier to the connection or not. The amplifier is what makes an organization prefer a connection over another one. This may have different reasons. For example, the managers of the two companies are relatives or old friends. This amplifier can be a contractual condition like the contract to work with an organization for a specific amount of time. This was labeled as 'bonds,' an aspect of relationships, which was identified in different kinds as follows: knowledge, technical, socioeconomic, planning, and legal (Johanson & Mattsson, 1987).

Looking at the networks, as mentioned earlier, they may be large or small, subsuming strong or weak ties, or they may be homogenous or heterogeneous. They are homogenous if they consist of firms that are active in the same sector, and they are taken as heterogeneous when their firms come from different sectors.

Interorganizational adaptation literature was studied with respect to two dimensions: technical and behavioral; the behavioral dimension is in association with the organizational behavior on the connection between the two organizations, while the technical dimension is related to technical elements like processes (Knoppen & Christiaanse, 2007). This can be viewed from a CAS perspective, pointing at the fact that after spending time in a connection, the two sides commence to share similar schemata with each other which these schemata, granted that they are the rules behind the behaviors, then cause the organizational behaviors of the two organizations to become more and more alike.

The selection of the adaptation modes is dependent on the context the organizations were founded in. The investigation of the possible modes in different types of networks can clarify the concept more. Starting with the size of the networks, small or large, the choice of adaptation will vary. In small networks, the number of organizations is limited, and for this reason, they have the opportunity to communicate with each other more often, making them become closer. As a result, the mimetic force is the most probable force responsible for the similarities seen in the patterns of organizational adaptation.

The large networks subsume many companies and when the number of companies increases, the communication will be harder to happen frequently. The lack of sufficient communication is expected to fade the role of the mimetic force due to the lack of enough information on the characteristics of the processes performed in other organizations. The most probable force is predicted to be the normative force since the organizations don't want to act differently from what the other organizations are doing, or to put it in another way, they would rather stick to the norms which look reasonable to the majority than doing what is considered strange and awkward. The power of norms should not be underestimated on many organizational factors such as commitment and adaptation. When saying norms, for some of the scientists with a positivist view, it can be underrated. However, looking at the real-world examples will help in the realization of its importance. These days, social media groups are so common among colleagues. There is no written rule concerning answering the messages; however, in one of the organizations, every member of the group feel obliged to provide a response to the messages within an hour otherwise he felt urged to provide excuses and make apologies for the delay. The other example is again technological, related to social media. Every employee of the organization with a social media account feels impelled to like every post on the social media page of the organization. These were just two of the many instances in which norms put the pressure on employees to adopt the same approaches. An exemplar of conforming to non-technological norms can be depicted in relation to the dress code of an organization. In this organization, apart from the dress code specified in the contract, the employees wear certain pieces of clothes with certain colors. The old employees have become accustomed to this kind of clothing as a norm. During the first weeks of the recruitment, the new employees wore clothes consistent with the dress code defined in the contract but not in agreement with the norms. After some time passed, it was noticed that some of the new employees have conformed to the norms for clothing. Some of them who could not conform to the norms resigned from the organization during the following years. The others still remain in the same organization. The factor that should neither be ignored nor underrated in the social studies is the human factor. The personality of people vary, so do their reactions, and each prescription and theory cannot cover all types of individuals. The ones still working in the organization might bear some characteristics such as the ignorance of others, being self-centered, or simply continuing working due to financial matters.

The next two discussions are concentrated on the forces of adaptation modes in networks with strong ties and networks with weak ties. While the size of the network is about the number of companies found in a network, the strong and weak categorization is in association with the strengths of the connections formed in a network. Within networks of strong connections, both normative and mimetic forces are expected to be active. The networks with weak connections are more prone to be under the impact of the coercive forces attributable to the lack of enough communication within them. They don't communicate and share their information with each other sufficiently which then deter them from getting to know the norms and the processes of other organizations, making the normative and mimetic forces less powerful and more ineffective.

In the clusters, the extent to which an organization is engaged in an industrial cluster has an impact on its adaptation outcomes though the advantages provided by the adaptation is dependent on how the engagement is taking place (Niu, 2010). The companies in a cluster compete and/ or collaborate with each other, and the degree of competition and collaboration and their probable interaction are some of the factors related to how involved they are with their clusters.

Bibliography

Abatecola, G. (2012). Organizational Adaptation: An Update. *International Journal of Organizational Analysis, 20*(3), 274–293.

Bak, P. (1996). *How Nature Works: The Science of Self-Organized Criticality* (1st ed.). New York: Springer-Verlag.

Burgelman, R. A. (1991). Intraorganizational Ecology of Strategy Making and Organizational Adaptation: Theory and Field Research. *Organization Science, 2*(3), 239–262.

Cameron, K. S. (1984). Organizational Adaptation and Higher Education. *The Journal of Higher Education, 55*(2), 122–144.

Carley, K. M. (1997). Organizational Adaptation. *Annals of Operations Research, 75,* 25–47.

Carley, K. M., & Lee, J.-S. (1998). Dynamic Organizations: Organizational Adaptation in a Changing Environment. *Advances in Strategic Management, 15,* 269–297.

Chakravarthy, B. S. (1982). A Promising Metaphor for Strategic Management. *The Academy of Management Review, 7*(1), 35–44.

Comfort, L. K. (1994). Self-Organization in Complex Systems. *Journal of Public Administration Research and Theory (J-PART), 4*(3), 393–410.

Daft, R. L. (2007). *Organization Theory and Design* (9th ed.). Willard, OH: Thomson Higher Education.

Faucher, J.-B. P. (2010). *Reconceptualizing Knowledge Management: Knowledge, Social Energy, and Emergent Leadership in Social Complex Adaptive Systems* (PhD Thesis ed.). Dunedin: University of Otago.

Fidanboy, M. (2020). *A Multi-level Study of Technoparks within Complex Adaptive Systems Perspective: A Case Study of Factors Influencing R&D Performance* (PhD Dissertation). Ankara: Ankara Yildirim Beyazit University.

Ford, J. D., & Baucus, D. A. (1987). Organizational Adaptation to Performance Downturns: An Interpretation-Based Perspective. *The Academy of Management Review, 12*(2), 366–380.

Fox-Wolfgramm, S. J., Boal, K. B., & Hunt, J. G. (1998). Organizational Adaptation to Institutional Change: A Comparative Study of First-Order Change in Prospector and Defender Banks. *Administrative Science Quarterly, 43*(1), 87–126.

Jennings, D. F., & Seaman, S. L. (1994). High and Low Levels of Organizational Adaptation: An Empirical Analysis of Strategy, Structure, and Performance. *Strategic Management Journal, 15*(6), 459–475.

Johanson, J., & Mattsson, L.-G. (1987). Interorganizational Relations in Industrial Systems: A Network Approach Compared with the Transaction-Cost Approach. *International Studies of Management & Organization, 17*, 34–48.

Knoppen, D., & Christiaanse, E. (2007). Interorganizational Adaptation in Supply Chains: A Behavioral Perspective. *The International Journal of Logistics, 18*(2), 217–237.

Kraatz, M. S. (1998). Learning by Association? Interorganizational Networks and Adaptation to Environmental Change. *The Academy of Management Journal, 41*(6), 621–643.

Levinthal, D. A. (1991). Organizational Adaptation and Environmental Selection-Interrelated Processes of Change. *Organization Science, 2*, 140–145.

Levinthal, D. A., & Marin, A. (2015). Three Facets of Organizational Adaptation: Selection, Variety, and Plasticity. *Organization Science, 26*(3), 743–755.

Miller, D., & Friesen, P. H. (1980). Momentum and Revolution in Organizational Adaptation. *The Academy of Management Journal, 23*(4), 591–614.

Milliken, F. J., Dutton, J. E., & Beyer, J. M. (1992). Understanding Organizational Adaptation to Change: The Case of Work-Family Issues. In D. M. Schweiger & K. Papenfuß (Eds.), *Human Resource Planning* (pp. 279–295). Gabler Verlag. https://doi.org/10.1007/978-3-322-83820-9_25.

Mitleton-Kelly, E. (2003). Ten Principles of Complexity and Enabling Infrastructures. In E. Mitleton-Kelly (Ed.), *Complex Systems and Evolutionary Perspectives on Organizations; The Application of Complexity Theory to the Organizations* (p. 43). Oxford: Elsevier Science Ltd.

Niu, K.-H. (2010). Industrial Cluster Involvement and Organizational Adaptation. *Competitiveness Review: An International Business Journal, 20*(5), 395–406.

Potts, J. (2000). System Theory and Complexity. In J. Potts (Ed.), *The New Evolutionary Microeconomics; Complexity, Competence and Adaptive Behavior* (pp. 83–108). Cheltenham: Edward Elgar Publishing Limited.

4 Application of CAS Perspective in Organizations

Case 1: Organization and Customer Relationship

A software company took an order to create a software compliant with one type of quality standards. The customer company did not have a clear understanding of the mentioned standard, only requested it in order to be able to meet the requirements of a project; therefore, it hired a consultant to help them with improving their knowledge of those quality standards. Similarly, the software company also asked a consultancy company to observe their current processes and to guide them through the whole project regarding the quality standards.

After the first release and demonstration, the problems started to rise due to the variance between the customer company's expectations and the software company's deliverables.

As of the first solution, the project manager of the software company held several meetings with the customer to adjust the list of requirements according to their requests. After several meetings, the project manager found it hard to satisfy the customer for the reason that not any solutions seemed to be adequate. The project manager approved the changes time after time; nevertheless, the feedbacks from the customer's side did not become positive. The technical team started complaining about the number of changes imposed on the project.

The second approach toward solving the problems taken by the project manager was to offer the customer to ask his consultants to meet their consultants in the hope of the clarification of any blurred insights. The meeting took place with the attendance of the consultants from both sides together with the project managers of the both companies. The first meeting did not end much fruitful as the consultants did not make any efforts to listen to each other. The meeting was mostly an event for them to prove their knowledge and experience instead of a tool for negotiation or reaching a compromise.

Already learnt from the experience, as the third solution, the project managers of the customer and software companies asked their consultants to prioritize the clauses of the standards' guide regarding their importance to them. After preparing the list, the project managers of the two sides held

DOI: 10.4324/9781003182764-4

meetings and discussed the priorities in order to find a common solution. This had not been made easy just after the project managers used the same system for prioritization and for assigning weights to each of the items, and at last, the final list was prepared. They, then, showed the final list to their consultants for their opinions. Even if the weights were assigned, the same meaning was not meant by each number. Hence, the project managers made efforts to convince their consultants on their determined list of requirements and it worked.

Approaching the problem from a CAS standpoint identifies the problem as the difference in the schemata of the companies originating from the difference in the schemata of the consultants directing them throughout the processes. The frameworks, models, and the standards are all for harmonizing the schemata of different organizations if to be viewed from a CAS point. Although the harmonization is the main aim, there exists the 'tailoring' or in the other cases 'customizing' whenever they are being made suitable for the use in a specific context. The solution to inconsistent schemata is to hold meetings and to designate mediators till a shared schemata or similar ones are shaped. The issue which cannot be neglected here is the process of selection of the negotiators. They should have sufficient knowledge of the organization, the processes, and more importantly a positive view of adaptation since modifying, changing, or even replacing the schemata are all part of the adaptation that occurs in the CASs.

Case 2: The Overconfidence of the Organization

The traps on the way of an organization toward success are not few, and they are not sometimes recognized. One of the traps in which mostly the successful organizations get involved is the knowing-all trap. This makes the organization become overconfident about the occurrence of success, and this may occasionally result in overlooking the changes that happen consistently, and the contexts which are altered from time to time. Reviewing some of the failures of big companies can be explained from this viewpoint. Even though, in some cases, the failure might not be directly related to the overconfidence, it might have been rooting from the ignorance of part of the whole of a dynamic context.

In this case, an IT company contacted a quality consultant for their project of gaining a standard certification and get accredited. The standard was not new to the organization and some of the employees had prior knowledge and experience as regards the standard. The consultant tried to teach all the relevant employees, irrespective of their background, the basic principles of the standard first. At this stage, the experienced employees attended the sessions actively trying to show their superiority in the subject, and they, from time to time, asked questions related to the advanced topics in order to prove themselves. The encouraging attitude of the consultant made the sessions so fruitful, and even those advanced questions helped with a better understanding of the subject.

After a few weeks of the practice and review of the basic concepts, the second training session took place. In this session, more advanced topics were discussed, and some disputes were raised between the new learners and the experienced members. Despite the efforts of the consultant to find a common solution and provide a reasonable answer to both sides, they remained unsolved. In alike cases, the remaining issues would again show up when the practice starts.

The implementation of what was taught during the training sessions started, and the consultant guided the members through the processes. There still existed some disagreements rooting from the previously discussed ideas. The attempts of the consultant to reach a consistency between the members in terms of their perceptions of the standard were successful, and the organization was certified and accredited.

When considering the problem from a CAS lens, it becomes clear that there were two main issues which the organization faced. The first was the high path dependency degree of the experienced members, and the second was the differences between the schemata of the experienced and new-to-the-standard members. Path dependency, as an important key factor of the CAS, should not be too high to result in a locked-in situation both for the organization and the individuals, and not too low, since the new decisions will be too departed from the previous ones, making the new decisions even riskier.

Case 3: The Customer Service Problem

The problems are not always present at only the production processes. All after the release of a product, there may exist problems as well at the departments in relationship with the customer, customer service. These departments, regardless of whatever they are called, have the responsibility to reflect the end user problems to the technical team; therefore, the problems will not rise in the future versions of a product or new products. Although three main processes of quality management, including quality planning, quality control, and quality assurance, are among the not-skipped processes done by the companies, there are still feedbacks from customers which inform the company of the failure in some features of a product or minor flaws occurring from time to time. These are not restricted to small- or medium-sized companies, and even large companies known to everyone sometimes recall all products of a special model or version due to certain flaws from the market.

The third case of this chapter is related to the issue which has been already mentioned. A software company had sold one of its products, and after passing some time, the problems started to appear with the usage of the program. There were several calls to the customer service in order to find solutions to the constant problems. The team at the customer service own some kind of technical knowledge; nevertheless, their technical knowledge is not as expert as the ones on the technical teams. Facing the cases where more professional advice and assistance are required, the customer service team asks the customers to leave their numbers and wait for them to call them back. During this time, the customer service team consults with the technical team, seeking solutions, and translating the solutions into an easily comprehensible non-technique language so as to discuss it with the customers. What should be noticed here is that the customers are not always technical people, but just an end user with the knowledge to use the software program, not more, not less. Thus, the role of the customer service team gains more importance in these cases since they are the mediators between the technical team and the customers. Rarely, the problems are hard to fix by this mediation role, and the technical team prefers to contact the customer directly to help them. In such situations, the technical team takes the responsibility to guide the customer as simple as it can be done without involving much technical processes. As of the last option for these rare situations, an appointment can be made for fixing the ongoing problem.

Looking back at the example casts light on the fact that the customer service team was not able to understand the technical team completely, and the technical team couldn't explain the solutions to the customer service team fully. The mutual misunderstanding between these two teams resulted in a delay to get back to the customer, and there were some more complaints. Viewing the case from a CAS lens identifies two main problems. The first problem is the inadequate or inappropriate connection between the agents of different levels, customer service level and technical level. Based on the definition of a CAS, the agents of the system are interconnected. Each connection bears two main characteristics: quality and quantity. The quality of the connection is about how well the connection is making the transfer of energy and information possible, faster, and easier. By quantity, the extent to which transfers are taking place via the connection is comprehended. It can be operationalized by the frequency of the transfers. With reference to the cases, the quantity of the connection seemed to be at the satisfactory level since the two teams were at continuous communication with each other or to say it differently, the communication was adequate. The issue was with the appropriateness or the quality of the connection between the two teams which appeared to be low. In line with the experience and practice, increasing the quantity of the communications is done much easier by managers comparing with rising the quality of the communication. One example for increasing the adequacy of the communication is holding more meetings or gatherings in order to share their information. Some companies, especially in IT sector, approach agile methods for this purpose, trying to implement them righteously while the others just adopt the concept of holding various meetings at different points of time during a project without implementing any other concepts of the agile methods. This might seem to be fruitful to meet the adequacy goal of the connection, of course, not the appropriateness goal. The quality of the communication is dependent on many factors including the individual factors, for instance, if a person can work as part of a team or prefer doing tasks isolated from others.

The second problem was the inconsistency of the schemata among the two teams. Many factors may have impact on the structure of schemata such as the educational background, work experience, job experience, and so on. The difference between the schemata of technical and nontechnical staff usually originates from how they perceive a problem. The technical staff views the problem in relation with the technical causes like coding problems whereas the nontechnical personnel focuses more on the effects of the problem. For example, a webpage cannot be viewed properly by the end users. The nontechnical statement for the problem is: 'The web page cannot be displayed,' and a technical statement might be: 'There are incorrect settings on the web browser.'

The problem between the Customer Relationship Management (CRM) team and the technical team was finally solved by hiring a consultant to attend the two teams' meetings, having him clarifying the issues whenever they are vague, by simplifying the technical terms, interpreting the daily user problems into the technical language, and easing the occurrence of appropriate communication between them.

Case 4: Top Management and the Technical Team

An IT company had been poring over different frameworks to find the most suitable one for implementation in the organization. The decision of the need for a new framework had been made after the approval from top management and the team coach. After conducting a remarkable amount of research, a framework was chosen and they began to implement it in their company. Prior to the implementation, the top management was informed of their choice and has approved it. The time for release and demonstration of the product finally arrived. The meeting with the customer passed well, although after the meeting, the top manager requested for another meeting with the technical team. During that meeting, he criticized the team for failing to do the tasks in the right way. The disputes were tried to be silenced by the team coach, and the meeting ended this way.

During the following weeks, the team coach made attempts to explain the new framework to the top manager and justify that the team had performed the tasks in accordance with the new framework. Despite the time it took for convincing the top manager, the problem was solved at last.

From a CAS point of view, the different schemata of the top manager from the technical team were the problem in this case. The meetings which are held in the organizations are just one of the many ways to harmonize the schemata in an organization. Organizing seminars, workshops, trainings, and other platforms to share the knowledge and information are also effective for this purpose. Another issue is that the organization is not the only entity to adapt. The top manager of an organization is required to adapt to the changes too. The learning should take place both at the individual and organizational level. In today's highly volatile environments, the managers are expected to update their knowledge frequently. There is another issue associated with the top management which is that they should have some kind of technical knowledge related to the products and processes of the company. In the past, there were many examples of the managers who managed the companies just because they were the founders. Many of these companies couldn't survive actually. Management is about both knowing how to manage and having information on what is to be managed. The lack of knowledge on the products, processes, and procedures within an organization can lead to mismanagement which can compel the organization to pay the price.

Case 5: Too Much Paperwork and Agility

As some words have negative impact on listeners, the others are naturally perceived in a positive way like adaptive, agile, and intelligent. After the introduction of agile methods to the companies, they, out of their curiosity, began researching them and learning how they work. Saying that a company is an agile company would have been considered a privileged characteristic. Apart from the companies that had investigated the relevant concepts absolutely, the other companies just imitated some parts of the concepts by looking at the other companies or perhaps, after looking through the methods. There are still some of these companies which just pretend to be agile, but actually none of their processes are executed in an agile manner. One of them was an online educational company that offered online courses to the students. The education market is not immune to the changes, and it has gone under lots of modifications due to the changes in technology. This educational organization intended to become agile so as to be more rapid in responding to the changes in their environment; nevertheless, a huge amount of paperwork was still present in the organization. Documenting is necessary, particularly for an educational organization, although recording everything on the paper demands lots of time and space. They intended to employ a consultant to take them out of this paradoxical situation: abundant paperwork and agility. The consultant suggested them to use the programs to record the information in soft form, and some of the information was automatically recorded at the same time as it was entered onto the website; thus, the time spent on the documentation was reduced. Using the program helped the company to make changes whenever needed without being compelled to look for that certain document in the archives.

Employing the CAS perspective to this case helps with the identification of several issues which are described in the following. The first issue is the imitation of the agile companies which happens because of the mimetic forces. These coerce the organization to adapt; though in some cases, the organization may lack the appropriate infrastructure. The second issue is the partial adaptation where some elements of the organization adapt, whereas the others remain same as they were before. The organizational adaptation is about the adjustments in the organizational elements wherever it has to be done. During some adaptation processes, only a certain number of elements should be altered; however, in other situations, all the elements should experience some kind of change albeit mildly. Even in the partial adaptation, the elements which were first unchanged will experience change at a time in future for the reason that the changes in the other elements have altered the context for their action and behavior. This is what happened at the example of the online educational organization.

Index